THE TWILIGHT OF
INDIA'S WILD LIFE

THE
TWILIGHT OF
INDIA'S WILD LIFE

Balakrishna Seshadri

LONDON: JOHN BAKER PUBLISHERS 1969
BOMBAY: OXFORD UNIVERSITY PRESS

© 1969

B. SESHADRI

First published in Great Britain in 1969 by

JOHN BAKER PUBLISHERS LTD
5 Royal Opera Arcade
Pall Mall, London SW1

Edition for India, Burma, Ceylon and Nepal
First published in 1969 by

JOHN BROWN
Oxford University Press, Bombay
S.B.N 212.99838.2

Printed in Great Britain at

THE CURWEN PRESS, PLAISTOW, LONDON E13

CONTENTS

To
My MOTHER
who first taught me that animals
were entitled to especial compas-
sion from Man as they were dumb

and

My FATHER
scholar and mathematician, whose
spiritual powers over reptile and
insect poisons were a never-end-
ing source of the miraculous in
my boyhood

LIST OF ILLUSTRATIONS

LIST OF MAPS

PREFACE

I HAVE IN THIS BOOK attempted to show the desperate position of the wild life of India; how desperate is known and understood only by a few dedicated naturalists. Wild life conservation is but vaguely and poorly understood in India, and there is neither public feeling for the animals, nor is the State keenly interested in the problem. Optimistic pictures are presented to the outside world, and it is one of the tragedies of the situation that authority feels compelled to present this front. The truth, on the other hand, may enlist world sympathy and make more funds and expert advice available, both of which are terribly needed to save the fast-deteriorating situation.

I have presented a strictly factual account designed neither to please nor to displease, without presumption as to exactitude in surviving populations of threatened species (where such estimates are possible), or any attempt to pontify on aspects of wilderness and wild life conservation. The greater part of the information presented is a result of personal observation and inquiry, but I have drawn on facts and figures given to me by unimpeachable sources or in published accounts of naturalists of established repute. Of the latter, there are many more knowledgeable than I am and better fitted to fight the battle for India's wild life. Sadly, E. P. Gee, who was pre-eminent in his knowledge of our wild animals, in their immense variety and extensive range, died in October 1968. There are M. Krishnan, naturalist, writer, artist, and redoubtable champion of the wild creatures; Sálim Ali, doyen of ornithologists; and others too. They are men whose contributions would have been vastly more appreciated in a different environment, and made use of. I have the privilege of knowing some of them and have drawn freely on my conversations with them which have enriched my own understanding of wild life.

I have omitted mention of many animals, not because they have not interested me or do not deserve attention, but simply because it has been impossible to consider them within the compass of this book. Much, very much more can be written. There are India's birds too, rich and varied, many of which are in urgent need of protection. But as my primary interest has been the mammals, I have used a representative number of them to present my thesis.

My searches grew from my extensive wanderings in India's forests over many years, and have been intensive in the midst of my professional work. I am an engineer, and with the opportunities for travel such as I have had, this in itself has helped me, instead of posing an obstacle, in penetrating remote areas, although not always in pursuit of duty. The seeking of wild animals in India today is an immensely difficult task, not only because they are scarce, but also because most of them have retreated to heavy cover or become nocturnal in the face of heavy persecution. Conditions like those in East Africa rarely obtain in India, and visitors even to the sanctuaries have often to go away disappointed, as they do not see wild life in any numbers, or sometimes not at all. Wild life needs to be given a sense of security to show itself. In this context, I have tried to emphasize that India remains content only at her peril to pay lip-service to internationally accepted principles of conservation without putting them into application.

I have given rather a lot of figures for surviving numbers of many threatened species, but only from the most reliable sources or censuses by reputed naturalists or my own laborious calculations, and none from official estimates, which tend to be too optimistic or based on past distributions. These numbers are changing constantly, almost always for the worse, but I believe they illustrate adequately the perilous position.

For the English and scientific names of the animals, I have followed the second edition (1965) of S. H. Prater's *The Book of Indian Animals*, published by the Bombay Natural History Society, as being the generally accepted reference work on the mammals of India.

I dedicate this book to the poor of India, whose unappreciated riches the wild animals are, riches which are being so thoughtlessly destroyed by those who believe they have no need for them.

B. SESHADRI

ACKNOWLEDGMENTS

My grateful acknowledgments at a personal level are due to Sarit Sekhar Majumdar, of Calcutta, Bengali writer of distinction, who persuaded me to write the book; the late E. P. Gee, of Shillong, Assam, the best known authority on the wild life of India until his death in October 1968, who encouraged me in the task; M. Krishnan, most splendid of wild life photographers from whose wonderful collection of pictures I was permitted to make a selection to complement my own; Dr. Terry Bassett, naturalist extraordinary of Lethbridge, Alberta, Canada, but for whom the manuscript might never have got on its way; Richard S. Fitter, Honorary Secretary, Fauna Preservation Society, who was exceedingly generous in finding me the publisher; and Richard Kensett and Patrick Kearns of Fotografia, Streatham High Road, London, who prepared the prints of my photographs for reproduction with patience and understanding.

The photographs in this book have been taken by the author, except for the following for which acknowledgements are due: M. Krishnan, 5, 7, 16–18, 22, 23, 30, 33, 34, 38, 40–4, 46–8, 50–6: Dey Studios, Darjeeling, 6 and 8: The Smithsonian Institute, New York, 9: *The Statesman*, Calcutta, 11, 12, 39: The Maharajah of Kolhapur, 24–8 (these pictures, of the cheetah, are from the palace archives and are over half a century old).

'One wonders that the fathers of the town are not out to see what the trees mean by their high colours and exuberance of spirits, fearing that some mischief is brewing.'
HENRY DAVID THOREAU

I

THE VANISHING WILDERNESS

In the woods we return to reason and faith.

RALPH WALDO EMERSON

ANIMALS WHICH ARE NOT DOMESTICATED simply live as they are meant to live in habitats of their adaptation, of forest, scrub, plain, or marsh. These are the natural homes that are being destroyed wholesale, the world over, as the human population drifts to an inevitable explosion. We call these animals *wild* animals.

This unprecedented increase in human numbers is rapidly and inelegantly unrolling across the globe in a way that would scarcely have been thought possible a quarter of a century ago. It is said that there will be twice as many people before most of those living today are dead. Yet, and in spite of the red light that is already more than dimly visible through the fog of the future, substantially little has been done by the governments of the world to stave off the impending disaster.

Nowhere in the world has destruction of the natural wilderness—the habitat of wild life—proceeded with such speed and totality as on the Indian sub-continent. It has been the most decisive factor in the catastrophic diminution of India's wild life—within and outside the sanctuaries—in the last twenty-five years. 'To destroy their[1] habitat is as unnecessary as it would be to pull down a great cathedral in order to grow potatoes on the site,' wrote Peter Scott, the distinguished naturalist.

This destruction of habitat is a direct result of the myriad development projects, great and small, which, in the guise of

[1] wild animals'

irrigation and power schemes, land-settlement plans, reclamation schemes, timber recovery and wood-based industries, plantations of exotics, or industrial and transportation systems, are scarring the land. The dry, unmelodious and intellectual husks which these projects leave behind them are the naturalist's lament. But his protest is unheeded and he is denounced for still hankering after beauty, an entirely unpractical lament.

Many writers have described in recent years, in books and in articles, the precarious state of Africa's wild animals. Radio and television programmes have reinforced their pleas for conservation. Leading naturalists have summed up the situation as 'desperate'. The state of affairs in India, equally outstanding in its wild life, is no less desperate, but has received little publicity and less attention.

In Africa, the three principal reasons for the decimation of wild life have been stated to be illegal hunting, inadequate game laws, and superfluous cattle. Pressure from human population expansion is only just beginning. In India, however, the deciding factor is the widespread destruction of habitats for human exploitation. Poaching and overgrazing by domestic livestock are important but secondary factors which take their toll—a heavy one; but they alone would not have brought so many species of wild life to vanishing point in so few years.

There is not the same danger, in scale, from tribal hunters in India, though in certain favoured areas forest-based tribes have in recent years successfully destroyed every vestige of wild life. The depredations of poachers chiefly affect animals of meat value like the deer and the antelopes, or animals of commercial value like the rhinoceros, the musk deer, and the leopards. Here, a reservation is necessary. The last two decades have seen the emergence and then an inordinate increase in the numbers of gentlemen-poachers, casual sportsmen who ride in jeeps and roam the jungles at night dispensing with the trifling formality of shooting permits. The time of year, sex, and age of the animals are all the same to them. But even so, the poacher, tribal or genteel, must be given second place when pinning responsibility for the murder of wild life, followed closely by overgrazing by domestic livestock—a deadly way of turning choice grasslands into barren wastes. I do not seek to minimize the destructive role of either, but habitat destruction through project work and what follows it is by far the most pertinent, and the one needing the most urgent attention.

Development projects, among them the river valley projects the most immense, pound into nature and leave it breathless and exhausted. The despoliation of nature is seldom quoted as a reason for the disappearance of wild life as is poaching, for instance, simply because of a certain conformation to past thinking. Poaching consists of a definite act of killing without legal sanction to do so, and is therefore readily singled out as inimical to conservation. The destruction of wild life habitats by submergence of vast forest areas by a water reservoir, or by clearance for agricultural land or human settlement, is carried out by the State, and the perishing of vast numbers of wild animals in these processes becomes incidental and does not make news. Neither does it seem possible for the naturalist to say or do very much when these acts of destruction—results of superficial thinking as they may be—are put to the public as entirely natural, inevitable and beneficial. These schemes are launched without regard for the natural associations which they supplant.

As a naturalist, I have watched, helplessly, the vanishing of the wilderness and the decimation of wild life during all of this period, the years following the end of the second world war. In 1965, I completed the whole circuit of India's more important forest areas, missing only the Gir Forest in Gujerat, where the remnants of Asia's lions live. But, in a way, I made up for this lapse by visiting the Chandraprabha Sanctuary, in Uttar Pradesh, the so-called second home of the lion.

The resulting picture in my mind is one of terrible devastation. Totally gone are some of the most famous wild life areas, inundated by vast water reservoirs built for irrigation or power or both, or cleared for the settlement of the proliferating population or the refugees from across the international frontiers on the west, north, and east, or put to cultivation to increase production of food of which there never seems enough (especially as the annual loss of food grains to rodents alone is about 30 per cent of the total production, as estimated by the Food and Agricultural Organization of the United Nations), or simply and directly destroyed by commercial interests. Expansive and pristine forest tracts have been levelled, lakes and marshes drained and filled. It would have been difficult to believe, looking at them today, that they ever existed as lush areas overgrown with tropical vegetation and providing natural homes for countless animals and birds, had I not known some of them before the transformation.

A brief description of the opulent background against which this destruction has taken place in the last twenty-five years will be of value. For this purpose only, I will take 'wild life' as meaning both natural fauna and flora, which it is in its fullest sense, in order that the fundamental and intimate inter-dependence of the natural plant life and animal life may not be overlooked. For the rest of the book, I find it more expedient to follow, as this is a book about present-day India, the meaning applied to it, for its own purposes, by the Indian Board for Wild Life, as generally denoting only mammals, birds, reptiles, etc. I also use the style 'wild life' favoured in India to 'wildlife' which has come into general use outside India.

Protection for wild life was known and practised in India over two thousand years ago. About 300 B.C., the treatise on statecraft known as *Arthasastra*, attributed to Kautilya, spoke of protection of certain forests with their wild animals, and rejected exploitation for timber, fuel, and animal products in them. In about 242 B.C., the Emperor Asoka's fifth pillar edict gave protection to animals, birds, fish, and plants.

For India, the hundred-year period 1825–1925 is the most noteworthy in its wild life history, as it was during those years that native plants and animals began to be systematically studied, and then scientifically described and classified. Before 1825, though the lives of men and animals in India were closely connected, perhaps more so than in most parts of the world, and animals, domestic and wild, held special places of interest and affection in the religion, folklore, and literature of the peoples of India, there was an astounding lack of natural history, even specific plant and animal names being limited. There was of course no taxonomy, and generic and familiar affinities were not recognized.

The credit for scientific study in the aforementioned period must be given to British naturalists, many among whom were amateurs only. A wonderful array of studies began to issue, of which examples are: W. Roxburgh's *Flora Indica* in three volumes (1820–32), R. Wight's *Illustrations of Indian Botany* in six volumes (1840–53), Col. H. Drury's *The Useful Plants of India* (1858) and *Hand-book of the Indian Flora* in three volumes (1864–69), Sir J. D. Hooker's *Flora of British India* in seven volumes (1872–97), T. C. Jerdon's *The Mammals of India* (1874) and *The Birds of India* (1877), A. Hume and C. A. T. Marshall's *The Game Birds of India, Burmah, and Ceylon* (1879), J. S. Gamble's *A Manual of Indian Timbers* (1881), R. A. Sterndale's *Natural History of the Mammalia of India and Ceylon* (1884), W. T. Blanford's *The Fauna of British India, including Ceylon and Burma— Mammalia* (1888), E. W. Oates and W. T. Blanford's *The Fauna of British India, including Ceylon and Burma—Birds* (1889–98), J. A. Murray's *The Avifauna of British India and Its Dependencies* in two volumes (1890), R. Lydekker's *The Great and Small Game of India, Burma, & Tibet* (1900) and *The Game Animals of India, Burma, Malaya, and Tibet* (1907), Col. A. Le Messurier's *Game, Shore, and Water Birds of India* (1904), and many others.

Simultaneously, sporting literature of the most valuable kind began to appear. Many became noted for the rich and varied detail of their observations, and became classics of their type. Examples are, Capt. W. Campbell's *The Old Forest Ranger* (1845), Capt. J. T. Newell's *The Eastern Hunters* (1866), G. P. Sanderson's *Thirteen Years Among the Wild Beasts of India* (1879), Maj.-Gen. E. F. Burton's *Reminiscences of Sport in India* (1885), Col. Kinloch's *Large Game Shooting in Thibet, the Himalayas and Northern India* (1885), Capt. J. Forsyth's *The Highlands of Central India* (1889), Maj.-Gen. D. Macintyre's *Hindu-koh: Wanderings and Wild Sport on and beyond the Himalayas* (1889), F. W. F. Fletcher's *Sport on the Nilgiris and in Wynaad* (1911), E. P. Stebbing's *Stalks in the Himalaya* (1912), and many more too numerous to list here.

Sporting experiences of the first quarter of this century appeared in some outstanding books of a later vintage. A few examples are, Maj. G. Burrard's *Big Game Hunting in the Himalayas and Tibet* (1925), F. W. Champion's *With a Camera in Tiger-land* (1927) and *The Jungle in Sunlight and Shadow* (1934), Col. A. E. Stewart's *Tiger and Other Game* (1927), A. G. Shuttleworth's *Man-eaters and other Denizens of the Indian Jungle* (1928) and *Indian Jungle Lore and the Rifle* (1929), Lt.-Col. C. H. Stockley's *Big Game Shooting in the Indian Empire* (1928) and *Stalking in the Himalayas and Northern India* (1936), C. E. M. Russell's

B

Bullet and Shot in Indian Forest, Plain and Hill (1930), A. A. Dunbar Brander's *Wild Animals in Central India* (1931), A. W. Strachan's *Mauled by a Tiger* (1933), and others of similar quality.

To illustrate the opulence of wild life even at the beginning of this century, I will quote a passage from a book which has come to be accepted as one of the most authoritative. In *Wild Animals in Central India*, Dunbar Brander wrote of the region of which the Kanha National Park is a remnant today, 'In 1900 this tract contained as much game as any tract I ever saw in the best parts of Africa in 1908. I have seen 1,500 head consisting of eleven species in an evening's stroll. It is nothing like that now, but it is probably true to say that it contains more numbers and more species than any other tract of its size in the whole of Asia.' As much game as in the best parts of Africa! Readers will be more familiar with descriptions of African game in the earlier part of this century—from the numbers of books that have been written on Africa's wild life in recent years—and few probably know that game similarly existed in teeming herds in India also. Again, more numbers and more species than any other tract in Asia! How denuded it is today! Elephant and wild buffalo, two spectacular residents, disappeared many years ago. Dunbar Brander was not familiar with conditions farther north of the then Central Provinces, but there are trustworthy accounts of the equal abundance of game animals in the *bhabar*[1] and *terai*[2] below the Himalayan foothills from the Siwalik Hills in the west to Assam in the east, and in Bengal and Assam.

By about the years of the first world war, the first signs of dwindling forests and diminishing game began to be realized by those most closely associated with wild life. There were signs that measures were being considered necessary to protect the natural forests and some species of animals which had become dangerously reduced in numbers. The Princes played an important part in these first conservation efforts, not co-ordinated by any means, nor wholly altruistic, but nevertheless leading to

[1]Deciduous forests with a small north-south gradient through which flow dozens of Himalayan rivers, tributaries of the Ganga, before entering the *terai* on their way to the plains.

[2]Long west-to-east strip of tract immediately north of the Gangetic plain, of meandering rivers, swamps, and thick forests (now largely gone).

the safeguard of affected species. They still did not discard their grand winter shoots, but their best forests became private reserves and were closed to shooting for all but themselves and their most distinguished guests, and the hunting of a very few species like the lion in Junagadh was totally prohibited.

In the British-administered territories too, reserves were set up, game laws introduced or tightened, and some kind of control was exercised. Rest periods were given to animal and bird life to recover in areas heavily shot over. Firearms were expensive and difficult to obtain, and this as much as any other reason prevented illegal activity on a large scale. In relation to what was to come, habitats were still comparatively undisturbed.

The position, then, at the end of the first quarter of this century was that, as the growing population was occupying more and more of the plains and the forests were dwindling, the wild animal numbers had been reduced from their former splendid proportions, but were still in no great danger, with the exception of a few species like the lion and the great one-horned rhinoceros, which were afforded a substantial measure of protection.

From 1925 till the start of the second world war, an uneasy period of semi-security for wild life set in. Forests and wild animal numbers steadily declined because of expanding human population and its minimal needs. But, except to a few, it seemed improbable that the once-teeming herds could be in real danger.

Real, large-scale destruction of wild life began during the years of that war. Forests were felled for timber and to make room for vast army camps. Troops entered them for training for jungle warfare, and the slaughter of the animals and birds began. Animals were machine-gunned in fun, and gregarious herbivores like the chital, or spotted deer, merely stood bewildered and stared in the direction of fire and were mown down. Surveillance was simply non-existent.

When the war ended and independence came, enormous quantities of guns and ammunition became cheaply available. The period of political transition was one of many uncertainties. Villagers who had lived, in the main, within the game laws, both from fear of punishment and lack of lethal weapons, assumed that the change of authority meant freedom from control. The weapons could now be procured. Forests were freely cut down for timber and fuel, and the animals and birds were slaughtered for food or sale of skin and feather. I have remonstrated at the extravagant tree-felling and been threatened with sickle and knife. Overgrazing of forest grasslands by domestic cattle and goats caused soil erosion; and as the Princes began to lose their political power, their reserves were no longer so closely guarded as they were before.

Upon this scene came a new and dangerous recruit to the poaching community. To the villager and the self-styled shikari[1] who was employed by the smooth city merchant to get him rhino horn or leopard pelt or deer skin, were now added government officials and townsmen in search of casual sport.

These men in the middle and higher echelons of society made the most of their temporary positions of authority or access to new-found wealth from war contracts, and shot away, from recently acquired habit, at any moving object on four legs in the jungle or pair of eyes that glowed in the headlights of their jeeps. With this leavening of the poaching community, poaching was no longer disreputable. These men were neither interested in what they shot as trophies nor cared to carry away the meat. They were too influential to be apprehended by the forest rangers, who were poorly paid and at the bottom of the official hierarchy. Thenceforward, the jeep-and-spotlight brigade became a regular feature of the jungle's night landscape. I have come across them, scores of these men, in all parts of the country, and sometimes heard the recitals of their criminal exploits.

The lesson was not lost on the village poacher, who was often employed as guide by the roving sportsmen from the towns. He came to consider poaching as a democratic right in the new, free society. None was apprehended when the forest ranger who reported an incident was required to produce a third-party eyewitness for the conviction of the offender. Investigating rangers were threatened with a gun or with physical violence if they persisted in their attempt to detain the malefactors, and received little support from higher authority. There were cases of rangers being shot dead by poachers. So confident did the latter become that piles of game meat began to make their

[1]Professional hunter.

appearance in the open markets. I have many times seen this in the meat markets of district towns, and even the butcher had decided he need no longer ply his trade in this meat by stealth.

There are extraordinary accounts of the period, even written into visitors' books in forest resthouses in tracts where all shooting was prohibited, by the gentlemen-poachers, of so little importance did they consider the restrictive laws. Some are startling, such as those to be found in the visitors' book in the Gorumara Sanctuary lodge. Gorumara is a pocket sanctuary of three square miles in the north of the State of West Bengal. The police officer who wrote 'A good place for shooting' must have treated the protected area with more than a certain amount of levity. His opinion was enthusiastically endorsed by another senior police officer. Another entry by a senior officer of the district had been expunged by a Chief Secretary of the West Bengal Government, with the comment, 'Expunged by me as it shows bad taste.'

Contrary to expectations, a few years after independence, a feeling of governmental responsibility for the country's wild life began to show itself. Side by side with the post-independence plans for immense hydroelectric and irrigation schemes, wild life conservation began to be talked about, and boards and committees were created to recommend measures for conservation. A Central Board for Wild Life (later renamed the Indian Board for Wild Life) was set up in 1952, followed by State Wild Life Boards in many of the States of the Union.

The boards and committees met and talked and passed resolutions, but as a thing apart from the giant projects which were already attacking the habitats. Similar was the attitude of the project-making authorities. Separately, development schemes proceeded, and areas of wilderness began to be cut and slashed without any possible hope of recovery. The tragedy behind all this was that, if nature and wild life conservation had been taken into account in the planning of these projects, and the work of the wild life boards related to their planning, both habitats and animals could have been saved with minimal loss and without affecting the benefits from the schemes.

New needs were thinly veiled as justifying the destruction—in the rare instance where justification was needed or demanded. In seeking panaceas rather than real cures—a habit not peculiar

to India—there was little appreciation of what all this injudicious use of land and water was going to mean in the future
years. A sustained attempt to understand development more
fully was lacking. A superficially promising way out of troubles
seemed the most expedient way out of the confusion of objectives,
and development activity was continually overlaid with political
tones. Destruction of forests and grasslands, depletion of the soil
with consequent exhaustion of organic resources, and waste of
plant and animal life were the inevitable results.

Development is a basic need to improve the lot of a poor and
hungry people, and cannot be resisted. Even in India, a land
long given to spiritual considerations, things not material make
far less impact on changing society today. Western traditions of
ethics—that they have to deal only with relations of man with
man—have been superimposed on indigenous beliefs, and
nature, in so far as it is noticed, is treated as a convenience in
a man-centred universe, with no downright value in itself.

Even so, scientific knowledge has recognized that there are
areas important from the botanical, zoological, or even scenic
points of view, where material (economic) considerations may
well have to yield place. In other areas of more or less interest
for economic exploitation—if such a thing is possible nowadays
—modern practices of wild life conservation could be put to use
and the evils of poaching and overgrazing restrained. Yet whole
areas have been ravaged in exploitation attempts that have often
only a partial promise of success or a limited number of years
of usefulness, or are even sometimes foredoomed to failure after
an initial period of apparent success, leaving nothing behind them
but ugly and useless land scars.

It is in the national interest to conserve the natural resources
of land and water, jungle and pastureland. It may therefore
appear that it is unnecessary to make a show of founding and
supporting a good conservation programme. The opposite,
however, is the case. The appreciation of conservation does not
extend to the politician or the general public. Immediate
convenience or temporary benefits obscure long-term dis-
advantages.

It is essential, therefore, to protect nature from such attacks
and so to ensure that some part at least of India's wilderness
heritage remains unspoiled. Project planning is concerned with

political and technical feasibility only. Wild life and conservation of its habitats to the maximum extent possible do not receive consideration, as they do in some parts of the world today—not always but sometimes—where there is greater understanding in this respect.

It is only the power, irrigation or industrial target which is dangled before the public eye, and makes repeated and variegated appearance in the project report. Execution is by a lawful agency, the State in the case of a power, irrigation, reclamation or land settlement scheme; sometimes a commercial group in the case of an industrial or tree-felling programme. The result is that, even outside the planning rooms, the wanton destruction of nature through such development receives no emphasis as the prime cause for the disappearance of wild life—often the two are not even connected—while poaching, disease, and other more or less important factors are repeatedly quoted as being the main dangers. Such an attitude is particularly strong among old-time sportsmen who tend to look upon all wild life loss as due, first, to poaching.

Planning of development projects should therefore definitely include conservation of forest and vegetational blocks which comprise the habitats of wild life. When such consideration is given and readiness is shown to look at other points of view, deliberation is sure to follow, and a reasonable compromise cannot be difficult to find. This will involve, necessarily, long-term policies like forestry operations, which will not pay quick dividends and, for that reason alone, go by default. A conservation programme will always seem unpopular, and therefore needs courage to propose and to execute.

Instances of merciless clearance of vast areas of prime wild life habitat are, tragically, many. In almost every place where a big dam has been built or is being built, wild life has been eliminated. (The Periyar dam in the far south is an exception, but it was built at the turn of the century and under entirely different circumstances.) The pattern and *modus operandi* of the dam projects is now a familiar one. Many thousands of men suddenly appear where there had been no substantial human colony. All around vegetation is rapidly felled for fuel and lumber. As the animals are exposed, they are killed by camp-following *shikaris* who sell the meat to the labour force, and by project staff who begin to get a taste for casual sport. By the time the dam and its appurtenant works are complete—this may take a few years with large projects—the natural vegetation of the surrounding area for many miles is damaged beyond recovery. This is a terrible waste of forest and grassland, particularly as it is additional to the tremendous expanse of natural vegetation which will inevitably be covered by the water of the reservoir. Wild life goes quickly, and finally survives, if at all, in little pockets of secondary forest, where the existence of large mammals becomes a menace and the obliteration of the smaller ones is only a matter of a little more time. The pity of these areas is that many of them could themselves, on the completion of the projects, have become the nuclei of wild life sanctuaries with their assurance of permanent water and undoubted tourist potential.

Also, apart from such direct consumption of habitats by the projects, their operational centres become focal points of the threat to wild life. It is from these points that shooting often commences with visitors being offered sport, and then extends without discrimination. There have been outstanding examples of this in Punjab, where project and operation staff, Indian and foreign, have roamed the countryside and slaughtered the harmless nilgai, or blue bull, the shooting of which is no sport at all.

I shall give a few examples of project spoliation from out of a long and mournful list I have collected. Herds of blackbuck roamed the plains where the Tungabhadra dam has been built in the State of Andhra Pradesh. I visited the area whilst the dam construction was still at an early stage, in 1951, and though their numbers were falling fast, remnants were still left. Poaching, however, was widespread, and all cover was being destroyed. There was, of course, no provision made in the building of the project to spare vegetation where possible or to safeguard the wild life from needless slaughter. Blackbuck meat was piled high in the open markets in the project area and in the adjoining villages. Urgent appeals were made for protection of the survivors. Nothing was done. When the dam was finished, all had been killed off. This happened in a tract which had been one of the animal's historic strongholds.

The Moyar river forests in the Nilgiri Hills in southern India have long been celebrated as a home of the elephant. With the

1 The Tungabhadra dam under construction in 1951. All wild life was wiped out in the tract when it was finished

2 Tea-picking in the Cardamom Hills, in the far South of India. Plantations were the first great consumers of wild life forest habitats

3 Tribesmen coming down from the high mountains in the Himalayas for the winter. Vast herds of their livestock make free use of the foothill grasslands and leave them denuded of grazing for wild life

4 Tree-felling in Corbett National Park to recover all useful timber before inundation of the Ramganga valley

5 Magnificent male tiger in the thick jungle of the Himalayan foothills

6 The northern Asian tiger is the progenitor of the Indian tiger. Here is a half-grown Manchurian tiger climbing a tree in the Himalayan Zoological Park in Darjeeling

7 Close-up of a male tiger, very much at rest, in the Himalayan foothills

8 A Manchurian tiger cub
9 Mohini, the white tigress in Washington National Zoological Gardens

10 Tiger tracks in the bed of the Ramganga river, Corbett National Park.
I followed these for many hours before I lost them in shingle

11 Champa and Chameli, the white tigers in Bristol Zoo

12 Tigers speared by Naga warriors and set up on trestles outside their village, August 1964. The carcasses are left to decay naturally

13 Tiger trap in Hazaribagh National Park

building of a dam on this river, and all the power installations
and roads and human colonies that go with a hydroelectric
project, and the cultivation that follows settlement, the forests
have been far more badly cut about than they need have been.
Formerly, the elephants posed no special problem in Moyar.
Now, with frequent human provocation and injuries received
from inexpert shooting, they have become dangerous. Naturalists, if they had been consulted, would have predicted this
response. Now the cry is for their destruction. There is one
favourable, fortuitous, circumstance. The Mudumalai and
Bandipur Sanctuaries are adjacent, and the elephants have
shown signs of appreciating the comparative safety of their
forests, and of retreating into them. But the two sanctuaries
have their own populations of elephant, and if the Moyar
elephants move in any quantity, the problem of too many
elephants in them may have to be faced.

The dam which is rising in Kalagarh on the Ramganga river
in the Kumaon Hills will submerge the loveliest and most
important wild life area of the famed Corbett National Park.
This Park was constituted in 1935 as the Hailey National Park,
later renamed the Ramganga National Park, and then again
after Jim Corbett in 1957. The territory of a National Park in
India is not inviolable even in definition. The valley of the river,
which demarcates the Park on its northern and western sides,
is of astounding beauty. I know the place well and have always
considered its scenic majesty as important as the Park's wild
life. The view from the crocodile hide in Boksar looking into the
Himalayas can scarcely be surpassed. In the winter months, all
wild life descends to the valley from the surrounding hills—chital
and other deer with the tigers following them. Visitors can hear
the belling of sambar and the barking of muntjac, and see
splendid sights from elephant-back. Yet this part of the valley
will be inundated on completion of the dam, and wiped out.
The tragedy behind this story is that alternative sites were
available, but as wild life and scenic beauty received no consideration in the planning, the present site for the dam was
picked. A high authority connected at that time with the decision was actually taken to the place by a senior forest officer
known to me well, and shown the extent of the loss to come.
The answer he received was that an equivalent area could be

added to the Park from adjoining shooting blocks to restore it
to its size, and that should do just as well. (This in fact is going
to be done now.) With this kind of outlook among the planning
and decision-making authority, it is clear there is a long way to go.

In Bengal, the disappearance of wild life everywhere has
followed the despoliation of forest, scrub, and swamp for development projects. The population, always dense in this part,
rose steeply both by natural causes and through a great influx
of refugees across international borders in the east and the north.
In north Bengal districts, railways, roads, airstrips, huge army
camps, and free exploitation of the forests destroyed the animals' natural refuges and eliminated migration into that region
from the jungles of Nepal, Sikkim, and Bhutan. The scant respect
paid by authority to the forests and their animal life encouraged
the increasing number of young Indian planters, who were
replacing the Englishmen and Scotsmen in the vast tea-lands of
the Dooars, to take to shooting as their major relaxation, the
labour forces of the plantations estimated at 300,000 men and
women to extend their illegal activity, and the tribesmen to put
their bows and arrows to greater use. In the central parts of
the State, forest and scrub clearance to find land for refugees
has wiped out wild life almost entirely; and in the extreme
south, reclamation and forestry operations encroached on the
historic Sunderbans swamp forests, and now threaten to trans-
form a tract that must be reckoned as one of the world's unique
wilderness areas, an extraordinary creation over thousands of
years of geological and climatic changes. Two great animals are
extinct in the State, the Javan or smaller onehorned rhinoceros
and the buffalo, the former disappearing even before this period
and altogether from Indian limits. The great onehorned rhino
has just managed to linger on in a very few pockets in the
north.

None of these large-scale examples of destruction has attracted
public attention, as there is little public feeling for the animals.
Appeals to stop shooting wild creatures, but none to save their
habitats, are made over the radio during the annual Wild Life
Week, generally by ministers holding the Forests and Agriculture portfolios in the various States. At other times, other
ministers hail the clearing of forests and wild animals as a
triumph of man over nature.

Development projects, therefore, are the prime consumers of forest and vegetational blocks. If their planning were based not merely on the political and technical front, but upon broader considerations of public interest, by a consultative process which would enable a decision to be made whether a reservoir or a new settlement is more or less important than the preservation of the existing features, then much nature and wild life conservation would automatically have been done.

Again, among development projects, water developments are of the greatest consequence to wild life, including fish, as affecting the largest wilderness areas. Every feasible provision designed to minimize damage to wild life and increase its chances of survival should be made. Water developments involve, also, watershed protection. Watershed lands must be used for forestry and grazing, but they are often the basis of subsistence for wild life. Ways of using forest and grazing land must be found which will permit the best economic use of the land without adversely affecting the water flow. Watershed protection to minimize destructive floods and sedimentation is an essential requirement for the continued usefulness of irrigation schemes as well as for the maintenance of the essential qualities of the watershed lands. Many of these lands are highly susceptible to accelerated erosion when the plant cover and soil mantle are disturbed. Not only does this destructive process reduce the productivity of the land itself, but the runoff brings excessive quantities of sediment to the streams, and these eventually become lodged in reservoirs and watercourses, reducing their effective life. Irrigation schemes being dependent upon storage and diversion of flows from mountain rivers and streams, the hazard of sedimentation will always be present. The deterioration of watershed lands can be held in check only through proper management.

There are large reservoirs built at stupendous cost and immense effort, that are now said to be in serious danger of silting up, by which the life of the reservoir may be cut to a fraction of that planned. One instance is the giant Bhakra reservoir across a gorge of the Sutlej river in the Siwalik Hills. The danger is said to be so acute that one group of informed opinion holds that it is in serious danger of becoming comparatively useless in thirty years, which is only one-fifth of its

project-planned life. The reason? Insufficient watershed protection, or denudation of forest and vegetational blocks forming
the catchment area of the reservoir, by which topsoil is being
washed away and into the reservoir in huge quantities, this
denudation at the same time doing away with the wild life.

The importance of such assets of wild life and fish requires
that a full survey of the project area be made, and areas and
refuges established where their placement, physical features, and
the project operation will serve to promote the development of
habitat. Where conditions permit in the reservoir operation,
reservoir drawdown should be limited to an elevation that
would provide a sufficient depth and area to sustain wild life;
or, if maximum drawdown is required, which would cause
detriment to the wild life or its habitat, provision of underwater
or retaining dikes, or upstream development to preserve
aquatic food plants for water birds, should be considered.
Reservoir outlet operation should release water from as close to
the bottom as feasible.

Reservoirs should also be used to create more water area for
water birds, which have suffered grievously from marsh drain-
age and reclamation schemes. Reclamation of marsh lands has
been proceeding and projected without giving any thought to
the birds whose breeding and nesting areas they were or still
are. The filling of the Salt Lakes near Calcutta is an instance.
These lakes, now reduced to some 40 square miles of swamps,
have provided excellent habitat for a multitude of aquatic and
marsh birds—over 200 kinds have been recorded—and additionally a forage area for many thousands of winter migrants
from northern latitudes. Great swarms of whistling teal, which
arrive annually in Calcutta in the cold weather and settle in the
lake of the Zoological Gardens in Alipore, leave it each evening
after dusk, fly the few miles to the Salt Lakes, settle there for the
night, and return to the Zoo before dawn. In the absence of any
restrictions, slaughter of all birds has been great, by townsmen
in the day and by *shikaris* at night waiting for the foraging birds
with arc-lights. Now the lakes are being progressively filled
to find space for the bursting population of Calcutta. Efforts to
get even a small part of the marshes set aside as a sanctuary for
the birds have not met with success.

A good example of a bird breeding and nesting area which was

saved is the Keolodeo Ghana Sanctuary in the former Princely
State of Bharatpur in Rajasthan. In its marshes, duck, geese, and
other water birds find ideal living conditions. Their numbers are
so great that there was no depletion through even the Princely
and Viceregal winter shoots of the old days, which collected
huge bags each day of the shooting season. In the post-independence years, there arose a grave danger from a reluctance
of the local irrigation works to let enough water into the marshes
as human needs increased. The marshes are dependent both on
this water and on rain water for survival as a home for the
birds. It was only through the strenuous efforts of a few, led by
Sálim Ali, that the situation was saved.

While great expanses of wild life habitat disappear, the setting
aside of tiny pockets of forest as wild life sanctuaries, as has
many times been done or is being attempted now in some of the
States, merely pays lip-service to conservation principles, and is
unlikely to contribute to permanent results. It may be better than
doing nothing, but these pockets are, in fact, incapable of
assuring what it is proposed they should do. Where a species
has already reached a stage at which natural recovery is not
possible and where nothing effective can be done because of
political and other conditions in the environment, the answer
may lie in saving what there is left and starting a nucleus
breeding stock elsewhere, as in the case of the Arabian oryx.
But animals which have not reached this disastrous stage are
penned into little pockets and left to fend for themselves, as a
gesture to wild life conservation, while their habitats, of which
there is still a good chance of saving reasonable expanses, are
allowed to be destroyed or go to waste. The animals in the
pockets will not thrive, or even survive, in these unnatural
conditions.

I will refer to two minute sanctuaries in West Bengal to
illustrate the point. They are tragic remnants of once lush wild
life habitats. The Gorumara Sanctuary in the extreme north of
the State is of 3·3 square miles. It is said to hold, by official
accounts, elephant, rhino, gaur, tiger, sambar, barking deer,
hog deer, and wild pig. Even buffalo is mentioned, but I
suspect that there are no buffalo left anywhere in the State.
The Chapramari Sanctuary, a little to the north, is of 3·4 square
miles. It is said to contain the same species of animals as

Gorumara. If the animals are there—and in one visit to Gorumara I did not see anything at all—what chances of permanent
and healthy survival have they, many of them the giants of the
animal world, and of great wandering propensities, in such
pockets? The honest answer can only be that they have none at
all. Neither sanctuary can, in the context of time, even serve
as a nucleus for the breeding of the animals, surrounded as
both are by open forest, tea-lands, other plantations, and
cultivation. Today, there is hardly any wild life outside the
sanctuaries. If the animals within venture outside their limits,
as they are said to do—and indeed as they may be expected
to—they are in immediate danger of being killed by planters
and cultivators, whether in defence of their property or not.

A graphic description of the devastation of this area was given
by A. C. Gupta, former Chief Conservator of Forests of West
Bengal, in the *Journal of the Bengal Natural History Society* for
April 1958:

A long tongue of forest running south from the Bhutan border
on the west of Jaldhaka river is known as the Tondu reserve
and it is in the southern half of Tondu (Lower Tondu) that
Gorumara is situated. At its north-western extremity it
touches the Kumani forest in the Himalayan foothills. The
Kumani forest, which holds a salt-lick in Rongo compartment
No. 1 on the left bank of the Nuxal Khola, has been for generations past, a rendezvous for scores of herbivorous animals from
adjoining Bhutan, the foothill forests of Kalimpong and the
farther end of the Tondu forest. There is no other salt-lick
to serve the animals of these forests. Up to the outbreak of
World War II the sanctity of the salt-lick was respected, and
many well-trodden game paths converged to the salt-lick
from several directions through the dense forest. There was a
large concourse of wild animals, elephants, gaur, sambhur,
cheetal, muntjac and others, to be seen in the precincts of the
salt-lick, and as an Assistant Conservator serving in these
parts some 30 years ago, I remember I used to be afraid even
to approach the salt-lick. The war proved to be the undoing
of many things, and the preservation of wild life was one
among these. Throwing the basic principle of management
of forests and of wild life to the winds, most accessible parts

of forests were heavily exploited, and large clearings were made all over for labour force establishments. This fever of unbalanced action lasted for several years after the termination of the war in 1945, and a very great deal of damage was done. In the context of the present subject,[1] the importance of the salt-licks at Nuxal Khola to the wild life many miles around was completely overlooked, extensive fellings were made in Kumani Block along the game paths, a large clearing was made fairly close to the salt-lick and a forest village established therein, and finally the Rongo Block in which the salt-lick occurs was transferred to the Directorate of Commerce and Industries for the cultivation of medicinal plants. It seems strange that in the Working Plan for the Management of Kalimpong Forests which was drawn up during the years 1946 and 1947, and which prescribed the clear-fellings in Kumani Block, no provision was ever made for the exclusion of forested strips along the permanent game paths leading to the salt-lick to serve as corridors. While dealing with nature human actions are often of far-reaching consequence, and the damage once done may prove difficult to repair. The facts enumerated above should prove that the actions taken over a period of years were based neither on a sound local knowledge nor on knowledge of the laws of nature.

Again,

Although this area was constituted a sanctuary nearly 20 years ago, nothing was ever done either here or in the other sanctuary (Chapramari) in the Tondu forest lying to its north, towards carrying out what is currently understood as wild life management. All that has been done is to exclude the area from shooting rights, and the provision of a small protective staff of men in lower ranks having no specialised knowledge nor training. The shooting right of the poacher, however, remains unimpaired, and a game sanctuary offers him greater attraction than a forest outside it.

S. Chaudhury, former Conservator General of Forests, West Bengal, wrote in the same *Journal* for April 1952, of Chapramari,

[1] Gorumara Sanctuary.

'Due to the very easy accessibility of most of the reserved forests in the Jalpaiguri Division, it is extremely difficult to protect the game there.'

My reference to these sanctuaries is intended to stress that a realistic approach is necessary to serious wild life conservation if the objective is to be achieved, and not to criticize the present generation of forest officers in the State who came upon the scene too late, but whose charge it is now to protect the wild life that is left. Sanctuaries that are sanctuaries only in name merely serve to draw attention away from the real problem, and create a wholly incorrect picture that wild life conservation is well in hand.

Wild life conservation by conservation of its habitats is by no means inconsistent with development and exploitation of water and other natural resources. It is merely that the objective of nature conservation should be kept prominently in view at all stages of the planning. Other considerations such as animal and plant ecology, wild life economics, and many more, have now begun to be increasingly debated and become the subjects of research work, mainly by foreign zoologists and biologists working in local laboratories. They are of undoubted significance and importance to the overall problem of wild life conservation. But it will all come to nothing if there are no animals left to conserve in the wild state, which is what must happen if the present habitat destruction proceeds without check. This is the inexorable logic of the situation. All primary efforts should therefore be concentrated to establish the principle of conservation of wild life by assuring countrywide mechanisms by which development projects are planned to take into account wild life and fish. Although I have mainly discussed water developments, as the largest consumers of the wilderness, the same arguments apply to reclamation, settlement, and other projects.

A brief general picture of land at present under forest will be of interest. In 1962, the then Inspector General of Forests in India, V. S. Rao, said that after the enunciation of the National Forest Policy, there had been continuous deforestation for distribution of land to the landless, river valley projects, plantations, grow-more-food schemes, and building townships. He wondered whether in view of these it would be possible to reach the policy minimum of 33⅓ per cent of the total land to remain under forests.

On paper, many thousands of square miles are shown as being under forests, but it is doubtful if any more than 10 per cent of the land is true forest. One look at many forests marked 'reserve forests' on signposts is enough to confirm that nothing like one-third of the land area could be described as forest.

Apart from losses through inundation and clearance, the practice of clear-felling without subsequent compensatory plantation has been ruinous. There is urgency in all this as the demand for wood increases rapidly and continuously, but the price in future years may be heavy. Trees and bushes are capable of natural regeneration, a slow process in itself, but felling far in excess of the recuperative powers has led to permanent losses. Large-scale conversion of some of the finest natural forests into softwood plantations and the introduction of exotics from Australia and other places are additional hazards to the conservation of native flora.

Natural forests are the basis of wild life, and without effective conservation of flora there can be no conservation of fauna. It is impossible to dissociate the two, and indeed it would be most injudicious to do so. Excessive free felling also destroys all under-shrub which is of vital importance to wild life. The extinction of many forms of plant and animal life might be traced to a disturbance of the flora-fauna equilibrium by human agency. In India this essential interdependence is overlooked.

Is there any means by which conservation principles and practices can be applied effectively in all parts of the country? There is, but a change of heart is needed to look at nature and wild life afresh. It is too readily accepted that as, under the Constitution of India, wild life is a 'State subject' (that is, the management of forests and wild life is under the control of the respective State Governments), the only means left to those concerned with the problems is to persuade a host of State Governments through their Wild Life Boards to do something realistic to protect the wild life in their areas. This attitude has signally failed to produce results.

The State Wild Life Boards are advisory bodies only, and are for the main part composed of influential rather than knowledgeable persons, where wild life is concerned. Moreover, in

C

most of the States wild life becomes just one of the concerns of the Forest Department, and no expertise is used in its management. In some States there are Wild Life Divisions within the Forest Department, but with service transferable within the Department from one kind of work to another, men cannot take sustained interest in wild life.

The Indian Board for Wild Life, which advises the Central Government through the Union Ministry of Food and Agriculture on what it considers wild life problems of national importance, is also an advisory body, without executive power. It meets once in two years, presumably for want of finance, when it ought to meet once in three months with the wild life situation so precarious.

What, then, is the means by which conservation can be brought into being on a national scale? The means is the enunciation of a National Wild Life Policy and the establishment of a National Wild Life Service. Many amendments to the Constitution have been made in the years since it was adopted. There can therefore be no obstacle to a rethinking on wild life, apart from the minds of men. No lasting results on a national scale will be achieved without vigorous and sustained direction from the Centre, and no effective management of wild life everywhere will be practised without the instrumentation of a National Wild Life Service.

The founding of a National Policy and a National Wild Life Service in another large country, the United States, is an example. There too wild life was previously in the doldrums. Their establishment was a saga in itself, and is well worth the conservationists' study. There too every constitutional and other obstacle was present. The disabilities were triumphantly overcome after years of struggle. There are now over 15 million acres of the country's most scenic land and richest wild life areas set apart as national parks or with associated status. Yellowstone, best-known of American national parks, was established by an Act of Congress on 1st March 1872, and was the first. The law which brought it into being laid the foundation for a new pattern of land use by which the United States Congress subsequently set aside millions of acres for preservation exclusively for the conservation of wild life and the pleasure of the people. In 1916, another Act of Congress established the

National Park Service, which administers the federal funds which are appropriated each year for maintenance and improvement of the national parks.

I have given at the end of this book a list of existing wild life sanctuaries in India, the results of the sporadic efforts made in recent years. Many of them existed in one form or another in pre-independence days as Princely or British-administered game reserves. Through them, wild life has earned a temporary respite from excessive human interference. Whether or not this respite becomes permanent and more areas come to be set aside for wild life depend on an appreciation of the value of the assets of wild life by the country's leadership, and the help, advisory and financial, which may be received from international organizations and agencies like the International Union for the Conservation of Nature, the World Wildlife Fund, the Fauna Preservation Society, and others. There have been signs of interest from such groups, which is encouraging.

Even in the sanctuaries, however, the protection offered is often only nominal. Poaching is widespread, and is a constant threat everywhere, including the better looked-after sanctuaries like Kaziranga and Gir. Local interest is apathetic and, with occasional exceptions, it is of no avail to stress the importance of wild life on aesthetic or scientific grounds. But little is being done to emphasize its economic value, by which the people may come to understand that wild life is of greater worth to them if kept alive in its natural home than if killed for meat and skin. This emphasis will take on meaning if the revenue accruing from the sanctuaries—still small in India owing to their undeveloped state—is applied to improvement of living conditions in the areas immediately adjacent. Simultaneously, it is also very necessary to educate members of the State legislatures to the long-term economic and other values of wild life resources, as, at the present time, it is entirely in their hands to set up more wild life refuges or to scrap those existing.

As one condemned to live in cities, I have continually invented opportunities to escape to the out-of-doors. I have wandered endlessly on foot, ridden elephant-back and on bullock-carts and camel-carts, paddled in country boats, driven in jeeps and a variety of other vehicles, and spent hundreds of hours following or watching or photographing wild life in all parts of India. I have enjoyed the wilderness in an intensely personal way. Invariably, when I have returned to a wilderness area, I have found it, if not extinguished, then stabbed and seared. Many places of outstanding beauty and wild life homes have gone beyond recall. I will end this chapter with two instances in a minor key, but poignant nonetheless.

There was a pretty little forest some miles from Jaipur, the capital of the erstwhile Princely State of the same name. It was the private reserve of the Maharajah, and I had sat up over a ravine many years ago through a whole night to see a tiger which was said to pass that way regularly. It did not come that night, but that did not mar the enjoyment of those hours. With my wife and our two young sons, I went to the same spot in the winter of 1963. The forest looked dry, dirty, cut down, and hopeless. A villager told us that there was no wild life left in the forest. We then went to the hunting lodge of the Prince, a sumptuous place which had a good collection of mounted animals and where I had been received with courtesy on my previous visit. Now we were rebuffed, and the door shut in our faces even though I explained that we had driven a long way and all we wanted was for the boys to see the stuffed animals, which we could see through the half-open door were still there. We left wondering at this change.

There is the junction of two lovely hill rivers, the Teesta and the Rangit, on the Indo-Sikkim border in the Himalayan foothills. This was a great beauty spot, described as a place of enchantment by travellers in the last century. In summer 1962, it was still there, only made a little more accessible by a *ghat*, or hill, road, but no worse. I had met my wife and sons there one evening according to a rendezvous we had made in the morning at our hotel in Kalimpong, which served as our holiday base. I had set out with an English visitor after breakfast and we had taken all day to descend the few thousand feet from Kalimpong to the Teesta valley by precipitous slopes.

We were all bewitched by the place. My friend and I, exhausted, had thrown ourselves into the ice-cold water. The waters of the two rivers are of entirely different colours, the Teesta the dark green of unpolished jade and the Rangit clear and almost transparent. The Rangit flows into the Teesta, but stubbornly refuses to consummate the marriage for several hundred yards before the stronger will prevails.

With the family, I went there again in summer 1964, once again from the same hotel in Kalimpong. We were going to have a day-long picnic by the junction. It was a beautiful day. The rivers were there, but the enchantment was gone. A vast, malodorous army camp filled the place. Why, we asked, had this particular spot, so well known, to be ravaged, when there was room enough for several such camps everywhere in the hills, with well-watered streams? We left, with little more said amongst us.

I have seen, too, destruction on a splendid scale. There is nothing I can do about it, except to write and record my sorrow at the passing of the 'wilderness and wet'.

> 'What would the world be, once bereft
> Of wet and wilderness? Let them be left,
> O let them be left, wilderness and wet;
> Long live the weeds and the wilderness yet.'
>   Gerard Manley Hopkins

II

TIGER COUNTRY

There is, however, one point on which I am convinced that
all sportsmen—no matter whether this point of view has been
a platform on a tree, the back of an elephant, or their own feet
—will agree with me, and that is, that a tiger is a large-
hearted gentleman with boundless courage and that when he is
exterminated—as exterminated he will be unless public opinion
rallies to his support—India will be poorer by having lost the
finest of her fauna.

JIM CORBETT

IT WAS ONCE the case in India that in certain parts tigers were
so numerous that it seemed a moot question whether man or
tiger would survive in those areas. This is not said light-
heartedly but as a statement of fact. Dunbar Brander referred
to it in his *Wild Animals in Central India* (1931), 'At one time in
parts of India at the beginning of the last century they were so
numerous it seemed to be a question as to whether man or
tiger would survive'. It is not my intention, conservation-
minded as I am, to plead for the maintenance of tiger numbers
as in those times! Indeed, the situation, slowly at first, rapidly
in recent years, has changed so greatly that now the survival
of the tiger in the wild state can no longer be assumed as
beyond reasonable doubt. In these precarious times for wild
life, what of the tiger? It is the most splendid of India's fauna,
and none who has once seen it in all its wild majesty in the
pristine jungles which are its home is ever likely to forget the
sight.

The tiger (*Panthera tigris*) is not a native of India, surprising
as it may seem in the present day, because for the last two
centuries it has been almost exclusively associated with India.
It actually migrated south from the cold northern climes of

Asia, and is still to be found in the *taiga*[1] of Siberia and Manchuria much as it existed in prehistoric times. After centuries of acclimatization, the southern Asian tiger is slightly smaller than its northern progenitor, and had adapted itself to the heat and humidity of southern Asia by shedding its long hair, while remaining essentially a cold-weather animal. Doubts have been expressed about the existence of tigers in India in Vedic times (1300–950 B.C.), and it has been said that there is no reference to the tiger in Sanskrit literature, as opposed to many references to the lion. From this it has been inferred that the tiger arrived in India well within historic times and is therefore a comparative newcomer to the sub-continent.

I had not the least doubt about the prevalence of tiger in Vedic times, even before I started to research into Sanskrit literature to investigate this theory, as I clearly remembered the word *vyaghra* which was never taken to mean any other animal than the tiger in all the years I studied Sanskrit as an additional language in school and early college. References to the lion were many, affirming its widespread occurrence in those times, but the tiger too was mentioned. I will give a few examples.

Chronologically, my first evidence is from seals, not from Sanskrit writings. Seals from Mohenjodaro and Harappa, the cradles of the Indus valley civilization, now placed at 2500–1700 B.C., have sometimes pictures of animals which are unmistakably tigers on them. In Sanskrit literature, the great Hindu epic, the *Ramayana*, is a substantial source. It is an immense work in verse, and searching for tiger in it was like the proverbial looking for a needle in a haystack. But the needle was there. One reference to the tiger is made in the story of the hermit's son whom Dasaratha, king of Ayodhya and father of Rama, hero of the epic, slew in the forest with an arrow, mistaking the sound he made in filling his pitcher with water as that from a wild elephant. Another reference is in the incident describing the coming of the *rakshasa*, demon, king, Ravana, to kidnap Sita, Rama's wife, in the guise of a Brahman when Rama was away. A third is in the description of the consecration of the new king of the monkeys, Sugriva.

[1]The great coniferous forest land of Siberia and Manchuria, bordered in the north by the Arctic tundra and in the south by the steppe. The *taiga* contains many swampy areas.

In the *Panchatantra*, that delightful collection of tales with a moral, believed to have been written down in the second century before Christ, there is the story of 'The Ass in the Tiger-skin'. But the stories themselves are probably much older, as is suggested by other evidence. There is, then, the *Suka Saptati*, or 'Seventy Stories', told by the Enchanted Parrot to keep her mistress from going out with lovers, for sixty-nine successive nights when her husband was away. One of these is called 'The Lady and the Tiger'. The date of the work is unknown, but it was known to have existed before the eleventh century. Many more examples can be given from Sanskrit literature.

There is also reference to the tiger in very old Tamil writings, which I consulted as the oldest of the Dravidian group of languages. There is further significance in this. The Dravidians were being pushed south by the Aryan invaders into India from the north-west from 1700 B.C., and therefore the tiger had also penetrated and established itself in the southern parts of the sub-continent in prehistoric times.

The tiger which lived in such numbers as Dunbar Brander describes at the beginning of the nineteenth century has, incredibly, so shrunk in population that I believe less than 3,000 are left within Indian limits today. It has wholly gone from many tracts with which it is inseparably associated in Indian big game lore, and for all practical purposes may be taken to be extinct in southern India. This conclusion has been corroborated by senior forest rangers who accompanied me sometimes on these trips, but some forest officers and those in charge of tourism did not agree. Individual tigers may survive here and there, Forest Departments may give optimistic figures and continue to show the tiger as an inhabitant of their sanctuaries but these will make no difference to the facts of the situation. On the other hand, appreciation of the true position could lead to the re-introduction of the tiger in the sanctuaries, and perhaps in forests which still have heavy cover and an adequate natural food supply. There should be no conflict with human settlements, or once again it will be poisoned or shot out of existence.

The tiger, unlike the leopard (*Panthera pardus*), is not successful in adapting itself to life away from the thick forests. It is limited in its selection of habitat by its way of life and its needs. Its prime requirement is thick forest. In its historic

migration south from north and central Asia, it settled in
regions with heavy cover only, and avoided bush country
—preferred by the lion—desert areas, and barren hilly tracts.
So it spread into the great forest belts that were available then,
unbroken for hundreds of miles in India, Burma, Malaya,
Indo-China, and the western islands that now form part of
Indonesia as far east as Bali. It seemed that it could survive the
heat, as long as thick cover was available.

The forests, again, were the natural homes of a variety of
large herbivores, the tiger's food supply. In every way, therefore,
the forest tracts of southern Asia became ideal homes for the
tiger, and in recent times its most important abode.

In contrast to the tiger, the lion spread from central Europe
into Africa and Asia, preferring to live in comparatively open
country. In India, it settled chiefly in the semi-desert areas of
western India and semi-arid parts like Rajasthan and Gujerat.
The result was that it was much more easily hunted, at all times,
than the tiger. Inevitably, as hunting became intensified, it
began to lose ground rapidly. At the beginning of this century,
it had gone not only from India, except for the Gir Forest in
Gujerat, but also from the rest of Asia. It was protected by the
rulers of the Princely State of Junagadh, within whose territory
lay the Gir, and survived.

But the tiger thrived. Lion-hunting was more favoured than
tiger-hunting, no doubt because the quarry was more easily
located and pursued. The lion lacked the cunning, the finesse,
and the caution of the tiger. It succumbed as much to its own
improvidence as to the skill and courage of the hunters. It would
think nothing of entering a village and a cattle pen or forcing
its way into a hut in search of food. It was less ready to slink
away from danger than the tiger, less ready to seek cover. It
was audacious and unsophisticated compared to the tiger. The
study of written accounts of various types of the last century
reveals much in the contrasting behaviour of the two animals.
Each little anecdote is of seemingly small consequence, but
together the incidents present a pretty good account of their
fortunes, their natures, and the ways employed to hunt them.
The popularly held belief that the tiger drove the lion away as the
more powerful predator has no basis whatever, because, firstly,
the habitats of the two scarcely overlapped, and secondly, no

one knows that an adult tiger is more powerful than an adult lion.

Tiger was also hunted of course. But till the gradual disappearance of the lion, tiger-hunting definitely seems to have taken second place generally. It was comparatively uncommon, whereas lions could be pursued almost from the outskirts of the towns of central and north-central India, and did not come into its own until the eighteenth century. But men in search of high excitement and danger hunted it at all times.

The Emperor Babar, founder of the Moghul dynasty which ruled much of India for three centuries, wrote in his memoirs:

> Early in the morning we heard a tiger howl in the brush. Very quickly it came out. Immediately our horses became unmanageable, plunging and racing off down the slopes. Then the tiger went back into the jungle. I ordered a buffalo to be brought up and placed near the cover, to draw him out. I also shot one off. When Khalwa Piadeh struck a spear into him, he twisted around, broke off the point of the spear in his teeth, and flung it away. After the tiger had many wounds and had crawled back into the brushwood, Baba the Yasawal went in with drawn sword and struck him on the head as he gathered to spring. The Ali of Sistan struck him in the loins. He plunged into the river, where they killed him. They dragged the animal out of water, and I ordered the skin to be kept.

The year was 1519, and the place the Indus-Khyber Pass area.

After the British came to India, many army officers and adventurers took to tiger-hunting as the supreme excitement and test of courage. Some of their hunting methods will send a chill of horror down the spines of the sportsmen of today, and the element of caution on which the greatest stress is laid in all manuals on tiger-hunting was singularly lacking. I quote from D. Holman's *Sikandar Sahib* (the life of Col. James Skinner, 1778–1841, a remarkable British officer who was in the forefront of fighting in the years of waning Moghul power): 'Some of the stories one hears about him are almost incredible. Baden-Powell in his inimitable book on pig-sticking, says Skinner hunted tiger in the way others do pig, with a spear, on horseback.'

But fatalities were common among British officers who insisted on following tigers on foot. Epitaphs merely record 'killed by a tiger,' but occasionally more is told. For example, a Lt. John Keith died of exhaustion two days after 'an encounter with a tiger at Syekherie on the Wurdah,' near Nagpur, while an official entry records 'died of wounds inflicted by a tiger'. Lt.-Gen. the Hon. Sir James Charlemagne Dormer, Commander-in-Chief, Madras Army, in 1893 followed a wounded tiger into a ravine and received injuries from which he died. A police officer named Gordon was seized and killed by a wounded tiger when following up, in the same year. He had forgotten to reload his rifle. The list of hunters killed is a long one.

As the lion declined, tiger-hunting extended. Hunters had necessarily to turn to the heavy jungles for it, but in prime tiger districts there were plenty of them, even on jungle fringes. Some of the early shooting accounts make incredible reading today. For those who had the inclination and the time—and there seem to have been many such—it was often possible to bag tigers every single day in any of the well-known tiger tracts. A Lt. William Rice shot 98 tigers during a single hot weather furlough. Lt.-Col. Thomas Bailie, one of the great tiger-hunters, killed 13 tigers in 13 days in 1820, and 50 tigers in Khandesh in the next two years. The old-time books speak of innumerable tigers slain.

This kind of unrestricted tiger shooting persisted well into the third decade of this century—some indication of the tiger numbers that were available. But it could not last for ever, and what finally put an end to the sport as it was known was the coming of the townsman-hunter who began to slay all sizes of tiger, disdaining to spare cubs or mothers with cubs, and who had no ethics about the business at all, such as most of the British and the Princes and their noble retainers had had.

Tigers are great wanderers, and even a single tiger needs many square miles of territory to lead its normal life. They follow their natural prey, the herbivores, which are constantly on the move in search of newer pastures and water, depending on the time of year. These movements became inhibited, more in some areas and less in others, with the losses in forest area. The consequence was that, as the herbivores got trapped in pockets of forest, the tigers stayed with them, and with the decline of deer, antelope, and pig, the tigers too declined, which is nature's way of adjusting the balance. In the case of both, however, the shooting, which went on without respite, speeded the decay.

The decline of the tiger may be illustrated by considering the changes that have taken place in one of its best-known homes in India, the great forests of the State of Madhya Pradesh, much the same as the Central Provinces of British India. The forests here, by all accounts, held astonishing quantities of wild life. Sportsmen seldom ventured into the dense interior of the forests, and enough game was available within comfortable reach of the cantonments and the residential localities for almost uninterrupted hunting over the months in which shooting was possible. Every greenhorn sportsman of the last century whose ambition it was to bag a tiger had his desire fulfilled over and over again in these forests as the animals roamed tracts as yet scarcely touched by man.

The picture of these forests has changed greatly, however. The great mixed forests west of a north-south line through Nagpur and the *sal*[1] forests east of this line have almost wholly gone, due to extension of cultivation and project expansion. In some parts, such as the tract to the south of the famous Khajuraho temples, the forests have become converted into useless scrub jungle through improvident or illegal felling, so that these areas are now no good for any purpose. As the habitat declined, the tiger also declined.

Then came the shooting holocaust after the last war. H. Allen gives a vivid description for this region in his book *The Lonely Tiger* (1960): 'Old-time sportsmen, had they seen it, would have been speechless with amazement, for almost overnight an entirely new kind of hunter had started to roam the jungles. There had of course been black sheep before, but most hunters had obeyed the rules and shot in conventional ways. Not so the new ones. Forest rules for them just did not exist and they shot neither on foot nor from a *machan*.[2] Instead, they rode in a jeep, and as it sneaked along forest roads at night they picked off everything that showed up in the headlights from the comfort and security of the front seat.'

---

[1]*Shorea robusta.*

[2]Small platform built on a tree, to shoot, or now to photograph, from.

As I travelled in the Madhya Pradesh forests and countryside, the answer to inquiries about tiger was often that, yes, there used to be many tigers in the area, but they had gone, though it was possible that a wandering tiger might make its appearance on occasions. In contrast to the townsman's unreasoning fear of the tiger, and the reports that circulate in civilization about its bloodthirsty qualities, the village-dwellers there, and indeed in other parts, lived in peace with it. In all areas where it had not been persecuted, it had not the slightest interest in humans and made every effort to avoid contact. Often enough the farmers considered it a friend. Their general attitude was that, with the disappearance of tigers, deer and wild pig became a nuisance to their crops. The tiger, left alone, kept their numbers in check. If the tiger were not man-shy, life in the forests would have been impossible at all times, for the tiger, matchless in strength, cannot be matched either in stealth. The occasional loss of cattle to the tiger was considered all a part of living, and a neighbour tended to blame the owner for letting his cattle stray and failing to bring them in before dusk. Owners too, as a rule, are careful of their more valuable animals. It is usually the cattle past their usefulness that are allowed to stray into the forest. It is the town sportsman who vents his anger against cattle-lifting tigers by his letters to the newspapers, no doubt in justification of his jeep-and-spotlight hunting of them.

Jungle people may see the wild tiger very occasionally, and make but modest claims, and the claims of sportsmen who profess to have seen it scores of times need to be taken with the proverbial pinch of salt. Forest men and women show no fear while talking about tigers, nor do they shun moving along the jungle roads and paths after nightfall. Their only security measure is in the long-drawn-out calls which each wayfarer utters from time to time as he wends his way along these paths, which is the way he keeps in touch with other travellers, who answer him with similar calls. This effectively keeps wild animals away—proof enough that tigers do not seek humans but avoid them. It is a familiar sound of the Indian jungle night, and a mode of communication in which I have taken part when dusk has caught me a long way from camp and on foot. It certainly helps to bolster up one's morale.

It is a strange but true fact that today, with most city people, the tiger has become synonymous with the man-eater. The depredations of a single man-eater receive so much exaggerated publicity that, for all they care, the beast could be the true representative of its kind. It is the old story of giving a dog a bad name and hanging him for it. From the point of view of the individual chital or pig, there is of course no such thing as a good tiger. But the great beast is harmless to man till it is pursued, shot at, and wounded by those who should never have a gun in their hands. When the tiger is seriously incapacitated by reckless shooting, and takes to killing man when it is no longer able to pursue and kill its natural prey in the jungle, the blame is laid squarely on the tiger. He is labelled as ferocious and bloodthirsty. The tiger may have no natural piety. But, left alone, he is no menace to man.

No man knew more about tigers than that greatest of tiger hunters, Col. Jim Corbett. He slew, almost always following up on foot, the most dreaded man-eaters that ever stalked the Indian jungles. Yet he had this to say of the tiger:

A man-eating tiger is a tiger that has been compelled, through stress of circumstances beyond its control, to adopt a diet alien to it. The stress of circumstances is, nine times out of ten, wounds, and in the tenth case old age. The wound that has caused a particular tiger to take to man-eating might be the result of a carelessly fired shot and failure to follow up and recover the wounded animal, or be the result of the tiger having lost its temper when killing a porcupine. Human beings are not the natural prey of tigers, and it is only when tigers have been incapacitated through wounds or old age that, in order to live, they are compelled to take to a diet of human flesh.

Again,

The author who first used the words 'as cruel as a tiger' and 'as bloodthirsty as a tiger,' when attempting to emphasize the evil character of the villain of his piece, not only showed a lamentable ignorance of the animal he defamed, but coined phrases which have come into universal circulation, and which are mainly responsible for the wrong opinion of tigers held by all except that very small proportion of the public who have the opportunity of forming their own opinions.

The tiger remains the primordial animal it has always been. It is being exterminated in India for five reasons: first, the destruction of its habitats by clearing of the great forest tracts which afford it its natural home; second, unlawful shooting; third, depletion of deer, pig, and others of its natural prey; fourth, poisoning, as in southern India; and, fifth, wholesale catching of cubs, as in the Palamau forests in Bihar, for sale to zoos and circuses. I have already considered the first three. I will now refer briefly to the remaining two.

In southern India, where the tiger is now virtually extinct, numbers were exterminated by a widespread use of pesticides such as folidol and endrin, which can be bought freely or are even distributed free to farmers. Suddenly, a few years ago, one heard of their use in the Nilgiris, Coimbatore, and other districts in the States of Madras, Mysore, and Kerala. The methods employed were to leave poisoned meat along the beats of the animals, tigers as well as leopards, or introduce the poison in natural kills. I have not personally seen the carcass of one of these animals killed by the poison, but have been told that it is agonizing, speedy, and effective. Other animals have died too, even elephants, after eating sugarcane or fruit from trees treated with folidol. It is an altogether terrible story, and protests were made, but apparently too late at any rate, to save the tiger.

Cub-catching in the Palamau and other forests in Bihar reached serious proportions in 1958. In that year, the sale of at least twelve cubs in nearby Daltonganj was traced. A batch was actually sold in the Daltonganj court compound at Rs. 15 per cub. A sportsman's estimate of the number of adult tigers in the forests of that district was thirty, and he reckoned that seven were being shot each year. With this and the loss of cubs, tigers soon became scarce.

In eastern India, the price of a cub ranges from Rs. 15 to Rs. 2,000—it is all a matter of where you buy it. The price rises as the cub changes hands till dealers in Calcutta's animal market ask for Rs. 2,000, or sometimes more as the supply begins to wear thin. It is clear from this who makes the most money— not the *shikari* taking a certain amount of risk in killing the mother tigress at a waterhole, or, as is more likely, injuring her severely and leaving her to die from her wounds, before picking up the cubs. The Calcutta animal market is a kind of horror zoo which flourishes under the very nose of authority.

Catching cubs is destructive since cub mortality is already as high as 50 per cent in nature, and as it invariably involves shooting the mother. An average tigress in the wild rears to maturity no more than three to four cubs in her breeding life of about six years, from the age of four till she is ten. Tigers are not, therefore, prolific breeders. There is one more last tragic fact to add to this. Captured cubs die quickly in the conditions in which they are transported or kept in the animal market, and very few grow to adulthood.

A word may be said, too, as affecting the Indian tiger's future, of yet another menace to it. Indian tourist propaganda enthusiastically invites foreign visitors to go to India and shoot tigers. *Shikar* companies, good ones and bad ones, guarantee results. The visiting sportsmen are given the best facilities —the choicest shooting blocks, and so on. The bad companies observe few of the ethics of the chase—there are published accounts of their misdeeds. But in no case are the visitors allowed to go away disappointed, as it is bad for future business. This form of conducted hunting has quickly grown in the last ten years, and, as may be expected, the forests affected are those which still hold a few good tigers.

No discussion on tigers could omit reference to two unique tiger tracts—the Kumaon Hills and the Sunderbans—each of which has a fascinating history of tiger lore. Almost directly due west of the lovely hill station of Nainital, in the heart of the Kumaon Hills in north-western Uttar Pradesh, is the famed Corbett National Park, first constituted in 1935 and renamed in 1957 after the great hunter of man-eaters, whose exploits are household stories not only to the Kumaon hill people but throughout India today.

The central Himalayan foothills and the lowlands immediately below them are one of the most famous wild life regions in India, and still contain remnants of a rich and varied fauna. The belt was not formerly easily accessible, and animals abounded, but with the widespread clearing of the densely forested and malarial *terai* in the 1950s, much of the wild life disappeared.

Proof of the once-abundant animals was strikingly brought home to me on my first visit to the *terai* proper in this region in 1958 by the reported presence of tiger in some of the larger farms, many of which had been in production for seven to eight years. Indeed, on the farm in which I stayed on that visit, my host, who grew wheat, sugarcane, potatoes, and spices, was almost casual in his stories of the two tigers which had taken up residence there. On another farm, one of the biggest, the farm manager, replying to my question, remarked easily that they had no need for night *chowkidars*, or watchmen, to keep deer and wild pig out of the sugarcane, the main crop of the farm—adding, after a pause, that three tigers which had decided to stay there did the job very effectively. No humans were molested, and the farm workers had no fear of the tigers they had occasionally seen.

The Corbett National Park extends over 125 square miles of breathtaking beauty, and is reached from the little town of Ramnagar, the nearest railhead on the North-Eastern Railway. There is a road drive of 30 miles through rugged country, following the valley of the Kosi river (another river of the same name as the better-known and turbulent river in north Bihar). The Park was difficult of access in its first twenty years, and was virtually closed to visitors, but with this new approach road was being opened up around the time of my visit.

The road enters the Park at its northernmost point, and one is soon in a wonderland of many-coloured trees, creepers and ferns. Place associations with Corbett add to the excitement of the trip. Here too F. W. Champion took his magnificent flashlight photographs of tiger and other animals. Every so often a *nullah*, or stream, has to be crossed, partly dry in the winter months, and the music of the drive on the shingle accentuates the silence of the surrounding forest. The visitor inevitably arrives at Dhikala, where the largest of the forest lodges is situated, augmented in recent years by more tourist blocks. Dhikala is on the left bank of the Ramganga river, which forms the Park's boundaries on the north and west. The right bank, divided into shooting blocks, provides some of the most sought-after tiger shooting in India. The valley of the river as seen from here is of surpassing beauty. All of this area will be submerged by the reservoir behind the 412 feet-high dam at Kalagarh.

D

The flat valley here, called Patli Dun,[1] is covered with *shisham*[2] trees and tall and waving grasses. The forest behind Dhikala is *sal*, with the variegated colour of the *sal* leaves, striped and circled in the white sunlight and cool and breezy even when the grassland is warm. Some of my most glorious hours have been spent in these *shisham* and *sal* forests, which also provided a stirring and memorable experience for my wife when we camped in Dhikala for a week in the winter of 1964. Our two sons, then nine and seven, had a truly wonderful time wandering, and it was ever their delight to pick out the pugs of tiger, the great plate-shaped marks of elephant feet, and the slots of many deer. Both were already familiar with the jungle, and had together had a singular encounter with a rhino the year before.

The waters of the Ramganga shimmer and flow past in the valley below, and their rustle amongst the shingle and grass is sometimes the only sound in the wilderness. Occasionally the silence is pierced by the cry of a bird disturbed in its eternal search for food or in the sheer joy of being alive in this paradise, or bruised by the agitated cry of a rhesus macaque, mistaking a slinking form for its arch-enemy, the leopard, or in sheer homage to the greater feline, the tiger. Around the lodge, human noises only mark the universal quiet.

Both animal and bird life in the Park are rich and varied, but it is the tigers that visitors come to see. Sometimes tigers cross the Park boundaries into the adjoining shooting blocks, sacrificing security to their roving disposition, and come to grief. The number of tigers is said to have been reduced in recent years, and this is quite likely with the shooting in the blocks and the disturbance from the dam site area. But greatly wandering and loving the warm, sandy bed of the river in winter, there is always a profusion of their pugs.

On that 1958 visit, on my arrival at Dhikala, the Assistant Warden there thought it was too early in the season and doubted if I would see any wild life in the thick vegetation which seemed to close in from all sides after the rains. It seemed he

---

[1] *Dun* is a flat valley, or flat plateau, in the Himalayan foothills.

[2] *Dalbergia sissoo*.

prophesied rightly, and in the days that followed few animals showed themselves. Of tiger there was little news.

On the last afternoon, the temptation to do a last and furious drive into the Park interior on the badly eroded paths was irresistible. It was warm at midday, and the probability that any wild life would be about was slim. As I arrived at Paterpani, well into the Park, two forest guards were in the act of putting up a rough *machan*, more than usually high up, on a tall and slender *sal* tree on one bank of a near-dry *nullah*, while two others were securing a half-grown buffalo to a stake driven into the grass on the opposite bank. A quick inquiry revealed that the Park authorities had initiated an experiment to see if a tiger could be conditioned to come and take a bait at a fixed place, so that visitors could sit up in the *machan* and take their chance of seeing a wild tiger come and eat off his kills. A tiger had taken a bait at that place two days earlier in the first trial of the experiment. There were still his pugs about in the sand. A second bait was now being tied to attract the tiger again. The guards ridiculed the idea that any self-respecting tiger would show himself at that time of day, but raised no objection if I chose to sit on the *machan*. Singing at the top of their voices, to tell the tiger they were going, they left. It was too good an opportunity to miss, so up I climbed into the *machan*.

The silence of the next three hours was unbroken except for the antics of a troop of common langurs who were sporting themselves on the dizzy tops of some far-away trees. Now and again one would fling himself perilously from one tree to another, and it made *me* dizzy to watch this dangerous trapeze act. An occasional bird flew past the *machan* quickly and silently as if aware that it ought not to be about at that time of day. The *machan* was far from comfortable for a leggy man like me, and it seemed folly to sit there for so long, with a long and tiring drive ahead of me in the bitter cold of those nights to the farm in the *terai* from which I had set out to the Park.

Then, suddenly and without warning, the unexpected happened. Down the forest path directly facing the *machan* tree came a big male tiger, his colours brilliant in the warm afternoon sun. He stopped for a brief moment to look in the direction of the bait, and, sure enough, there was another meal there. Jumping lightly on the sandy bed of the *nullah*, he walked across my front towards the buffalo, which was fast asleep and mercifully unaware of its impending and terrible fate. The killing was accomplished with a light leap to the neck and shoulders of the victim, which bleated twice before succumbing.

The tiger remained in this position for several minutes, perhaps accustomed to retaining his hold on wild prey, before he began a long tug-of-war to detach the kill from the stake. The tremendous tugs seemed to produce no result, and the tiger paused several times as if to debate what it was that resisted even his great strength. The leg with which the buffalo had been tied to the stake finally broke off, and the tiger picked up the prize in his mouth. He turned and began to cross the *nullah* towards the *machan*. Whether it was the clicking of my camera or some other noise which disturbed him, he suddenly dropped the kill on the *nullah* bed by the near bank, and in a bound or two disappeared behind the tree, where there was a knoll of tall, waving grass. He showed himself twice in clearings, but I soon lost him completely. After a wait of several minutes, I had no choice but to start getting down the tree and steal back to my jeep.

Some years later, I heard that the tiger-training had been discontinued after a nasty incident. Some oversea visitors had sat up on the very same *machan*, which had been enlarged, later in the same season of my visit, and sure enough the tiger had come to eat off a buffalo he had previously killed. The visitors had been drinking immoderately during the waiting period and, whether or not from inebriation, started to hurl the empty bottles at the tiger, who was too far away to be hit but resented the treatment. He had taken himself off the kill, roared and roared again, and charged the tree, up which he tried to heave himself. The visitors had been scared to death, at this sight of a tiger climbing a tree. (Tigers do climb trees, contrary to popular belief, though they cannot be said to be fond of doing so.) The tiger had given up after some time, and gone away roaring. The story had come out after their return to camp and the site had been examined by an Assistant Warden.

The experiment was then given up. It seemed an unfortunate close to a clever attempt at tiger-training by which visitors, who primarily visit the Park to see tiger but seldom do, would have been enabled to see a real wild tiger. When I was in the Park again in winter 1964 with my family, the Warden of Uttar Pradesh National Parks, Naresh Singh, arrived there towards the end of our stay. I was pleased to hear from him that he proposed to resume the training, and would post a ranger on the *machan* with each party of visitors. I had in fact suggested this in a letter I wrote to the then Chief Game Warden, S. S. Negi, after my first visit, anticipating panic or irresponsible behaviour from visitors, most of whom would be without any knowledge of the forest or its animals.

The Warden generously offered to make a start immediately in the hope of showing my wife and the boys a glimpse of tiger, of which they were incessantly talking. My efforts to find one had failed. Two days before, I had picked up and followed the tracks of a big male tiger on the river bed and through reed beds, for a whole morning, only to lose it in a wide bed of shingle.

We thanked him and agreed to extend our stay by a day. A string of baits was tied up at likely places. However, there was no news of a kill for the next twenty-four hours. On the last morning, as we were loading the car for the long drive to Lucknow, our next halt, news was brought by a tracker that a bait had been taken. The Warden and we climbed hastily on two riding elephants, descended to the river bed and pushed through the *shisham* jungle to where the kill lay. But it had been dragged farther into very dense bush, and the drag marks were clearly visible. We beat the bush carefully and thoroughly with the help of the elephants, but of the tiger there was no sign. We returned disappointed, the boys most of all. Two months later, when I was again in Lucknow, the Warden's headquarters, I ran into him in my hotel. He said the tiger had in fact been lying very near, and had been located a couple of hours after we had left. It was another instance of the unexpected in the wild.

In the Kumaon Hills and the submontane strips of the *bhabar* and *terai*, Jim Corbett's is a venerated name. Leaving the Park, in 1964, we drove through the almost unbroken forest which stretches from the Park to Haldwani, along that famous, seemingly unending road on which he trudged times without number in peaceful pursuits or preparatory to the chase of that most dreaded of all animals, the man-eating tiger. We were broodingly conscious of the tragedies that had occurred with an appalling inevitability in places on our route, such as in the little village of Mohan, just beyond the eastern edge of the Park. Here, in the oat-grass of the upper slopes of the long ridge which falls steeply in a series of rock cliffs to the Kosi river below, had started the reign of terror of the tiger which became known as the Mohan man-eater. We were, too, constantly constructing mental pictures of one or other of his fantastic stalks after man-eaters, or his encounters with the mighty Bachelor of Powalgarh[1] as we drove through the forest block of that name.

I have been in no other area so permeated with the personality of a naturalist-sportsman. Impenetrable forest till a hundred years ago, and given up entirely to wild animals, much of the forest had already gone when Corbett arrived on the scene. But to us, the hillsides and forests seemed much as he had described them in his books. The forest was *sal*, and had the variegated speckled beauty of all *sal* forests. A profusion of ant-hills lined the road on both sides, and scores more were in the forests, exciting our boys to the possibility of snakes, big and venomous of course, issuing from them for the especial purpose of barring our way, and consequently for their entertainment. We passed hillfolk on the road and in the forest, gathering sticks and fallen wood for the home fires. The women brimmed with vitality, as they swung along in their multicoloured and multi-pleated skirts, with the rich brown of their skins to show off the colours, to the jangle of bracelets and anklets, and overloaded with bead necklaces. Tiny urchins carried packs as big as themselves, yet did not let the burden impede the joys of mischief.

As we entered the hamlet of Kaladhungi, we started to look out for Corbett's house, familiar from his own descriptions. Almost by a sixth sense, we stopped before a pair of gates, and within was a whitewashed and dilapidated house which showed partly through the deep foliage of the trees in the compound. Yes, this was it, a passing hillman reverently confirmed, when we asked him.

We entered the gates and walked up to the verandah of the house—the verandah on which Corbett and his sister Maggie

[1] A huge tiger that was the most sought-after big game trophy in the United Provinces (the present Uttar Pradesh) from 1920 to 1930. Finally shot by Corbett after tremendous tussles. Measured 10 feet 7 inches over curves (roughly 10 feet between pegs), a truly enormous tiger.

had received the news of so many man-kills or hastened to administer succour and treat the grievous injuries of their beloved hillfolk who, with a permanent assurance of the kindness and expert attention they would receive on this particular verandah, had so often found their way to it. After the sentimental first few minutes, we peered into the rooms through the shut and decaying windows, and a sorry state of dilapidation they presented. The property, we were told by the caretaker's wife, had been bought by a townsman who did not live there. The rooms were littered with rubbish, and peeling plaster and splintering woodwork completed the dismal picture. The caretaker who had the key to the house was away, and so we could not enter the rooms. We walked round the house, the grounds of which were neatly kept by the hillmen who lived in the outhouses as tenant-labourers.

Here, we thought, was an outstanding case for a national monument—for how many, among the legions of men for whom monuments are built, lived as he did, so little for himself and so much for others, simply, and giving help and succour to the humble folk around him at all times and at such deadly peril to himself?

Two years later, and over twenty after Corbett's death, somebody did work the miracle, and early in 1967 the Uttar Pradesh Government acquired the property and announced its intention of restoring the house and setting up a Corbett Museum there. An appeal followed for Corbett mementoes, trophies, and papers for incorporation into the museum.

Behind the house was an enchanting scene of green fields backed by heavy forest, with a distant line of hills, purple in the afternoon sun. The time came for us to depart, and we wondered at the quality of the man who had devoted himself to an alien people and received gratitude. As we left the village, we saw the walls around it which Corbett had built from his own meagre resources to keep out wild pig which constantly ran in from the surrounding forest and destroyed the hillmen's crops. The masonry, and the deodar, alder, and cypress trees in the village seemed to stand in silent tribute. To our stimulated minds, each stone of the walls stood as if a prince had scattered largesse; and largesse it must have seemed to the poor folk, assured of their meagre crop from the tiny patches of field to which each family claimed possession. Time will erase the stonework, and it will moulder and crumble. But it will not erase the memory of a good and brave man in Kumaon.

In Kumaon as elsewhere, forest officers sometimes assume an increase in tiger population in the reserve forests based either on the fewer tigers shot or more tigers seen. This reasoning is fallacious, as, in tracts such as the *terai*, the habitat has drastically changed from heavy, steaming forest to pockets of underbrush in the middle of vast farmlands. Not all farmers take kindly to tigers; in fact tolerance for them is rare, particularly as many of the largest farms have been acquired by retired civil or army officers, the former believing that all tigers are extremely dangerous and the latter that they are legitimate game wherever met with. The tigers shot by these men are not recorded in official statistics. On the farm of my friend where I had stayed on my first visit to the *terai*, his teenage son shot a half-grown male tiger which had presumably strayed in from the neighbour-hood a couple of years after my visit. In the conditions in which the tigers survive amidst these farmlands, their ultimate destruc-tion is a foregone conclusion. Some become famished and turn to cattle-killing, thus inviting even earlier attention from the farmers. Living in the vicinity of the farms, tigers are seen more than when they lived in deep forest, but an assumption of an increase in numbers for this reason is not justified.

Not far from the city of Calcutta lies another famous home of the tiger. It is a unique tract of country, doomed now to dis-appear as it existed for the most part, thanks to reclamation, settlement, and forestry schemes. These vast and lonely swamp-jungles form the incredible mouth of the great Ganga-Brahma-putra river system, and are the Sunderbans, a corruption of the Sanskrit *sundaravana*, or 'beautiful forest'—such it had seemed to the waves of invaders who entered India from the north-west in the second millennium before Christ.

It was a vast unbroken swamp region of 6,526 square miles, lying between the Tetulia river in the east and the Hooghly —which flows through Calcutta—in the west. Up to 28 August 1947, it was under a single forest charge called the Sunderbans Division. With the partition of the sub-continent, the western portion was awarded to India by the Radcliffe Commission, and became a new forest charge. The major part went to East

Pakistan. The reserve forests in the Indian portion now comprise 1,629 square miles, and are bounded by lands settled for cultivation on the north and west, by rivers on the east, and by the Bay of Bengal on the south. The tract extends 66 miles east to west, with a width varying from as little as one-and-a-half to as much as 44 miles. A good part of the reserve forests has now, however, been reduced to scrub.

The tract as it was (and parts still are) comprised a fantastic network of rivers, channels, and creeks with countless flat islands scattered everywhere. About two-fifths was under water, which is saline. No drinking water can be had except from rainwater pans. The land is covered with mangrove and evergreen jungle, which sheltered a rich and varied fauna, which at one time included the smaller onehorned rhinoceros and the buffalo. Geologists say that the formation of the Sunderbans is of comparatively recent origin. Even about two or three thousand years ago the whole area is believed to have been under water. The Sunderbans delta was formed rapidly with the change of the main course of the Ganga from the Bhagirathi to the Bhairab and thence to the Padma, before the sixteenth century. It was still untouched when men like A. W. Strachan saw it earlier in this century. He wrote in his book *Mauled by a Tiger* (1933):

If a gigantic spider's web, covering an area of approximately 5,340 square miles (158 miles long and 75 at its broadest) can be pictured, some slight idea may be formed as to what this extraordinary network of waterways is like, but there is, of course, none of the beautiful symmetry of our commonest insects to be seen in this enormous maze. The largest channels (fourteen in number) are broad and deep, opening out into lake-like expanses here and there; others, again, are mere ditches that could almost be jumped across. A few of the islands formed by these ramifications are as much as ten miles or more across, others as little as ten yards.

Covered with dense and almost impenetrable jungle in most parts, this malarious and sparsely inhabited region is the haunt of a great variety of animals. Tigers are particularly numerous, and dispute possession of the islands with the ponderous rhinoceros, while buffalo, deer of many kinds, and a host of smaller beasts make this portion of our Indian Empire one of the most interesting from the point of view of the naturalist and the sportsman. Reptiles, too, are well represented by the huge pythons and many of the poisonous snakes, while the channels are infested by 'muggers,' or crocodiles.

Such was the Sunderbans. Today, only parts of this unique tract remain in their original unspoilt state. Steady inroads were already being made before 1947. Now, on the Indian side, whole areas have been deforested, others reclaimed, and yet others forcibly occupied by displaced populations. The pressure from increase in human numbers in and around Calcutta is immense, and it may be that there is no other way out than to do away with most of the swamp-forests. Wild life has disappeared with great rapidity. There is heavy poaching as the borders of settled land move continually forestward. Only three sanctuaries exist, Sajnakhali for birds, and two terminal islands, Lothian Island and Halliday Island, of fifteen and two square miles respectively. I have unfortunately no information on the conditions in the larger part of the Sunderbans in East Pakistan.

But there are tigers still in the Indian Sunderbans. Sunderbans has long been known for its big-sized and splendidly coloured tigers—the so-called Royal Bengal Tiger. But their ways of life have drastically changed. As their natural prey, deer and pig, disappeared, the tigers turned first to cattle-killing, and then in desperation to man-killing. For many years now, all Sunderbans tigers have been assumed to be man-eaters, and those seeking information from the Forest Department are clearly told so. Man-killing does regularly take place.

This—the man-killing propensity—is now a main point of interest attaching to the Sunderbans tigers. Man-killing has been recorded for a long time, even before the present pressure on the tract. So the question may be asked how it is that these tigers have taken to this unnatural mode of living. No conclusive answer can be given, but my own observations, from visits to the tract, talks with the villagers, and the circumstances in which the kills have taken place, leave me in little doubt as to the pattern.

I trace it to a lack of the tiger's natural food. Both the thick

cover and the once-plentiful deer and pig led to the establishment of a large, thriving tiger population. As the deer and pig
decreased from excessive poaching—cartloads of their carcases
used to be brought, for many years, to Calcutta—the tigers had
to find something to eat.

A hungry tiger can eat up to 50 pounds of meat in a day. But
it does not eat every day. The average daily need is 10 to 15
pounds. At this rate, a tiger consumes 3,650 to 5,500 pounds of
meat a year, a prodigious amount. As there are inedible parts
in its kills, it would kill about half as much again in weight. The
time came, therefore, when there were not enough deer and pig
left to support the large tiger population. Wandering is the
tigers' natural propensity, but now they took to an even greater
amount of roving in search of food. Inevitably, they arrived at
the fringes of the settlements. There, they began to take cattle.
And who could blame them? They were deprived by man of the
food allotted to them in the natural order of things and, to
survive, they began to feed off man's domesticated animals.

This, just as inevitably, brought them into conflict with the
herdsmen who, while attempting to protect their charges,
occasionally got killed themselves. The tigers were not interested
in them as food to start with. But soon they got a taste of human
flesh as more herdsmen were killed. They discovered the ease
with which human beings could be disposed of. From there, it
was but a short step before they took to repeating the human
killings to obtain food with the minimum effort. A pattern was
established.

As the mother tigress taught her cubs the art of hunting
—Corbett found that this was a carefully contrived process—the
hunting of man became part of this process, and the habit of
man-killing was passed on from one generation of tigers to the
next. A race of man-eating tigers became permanently established.

The Sunderbans tigers will never, now, be weaned from this
habit. Additionally, in the Sunderbans, plying their various
occupations, are honey-gatherers, woodcutters, and fishermen,
who are often left isolated when the tidal jungles are inundated
twice each day. They fall readily to the hungry tigers, which,
without their natural food, expect and wait for such victims.
In the meantime, pressure for the destruction of the tigers

increases and *shikaris* are officially encouraged to undertake their shooting.

There are two other matters concerning the Sunderbans tigers about which there has been much speculation. They are the origin of the name 'Royal Bengal Tiger', given to large specimens in eastern India and particularly Bengal, and the occurrence of the animal in the great swamps, which are unlike all its other habitats not only because of their terrain but also of the salinity of the water everywhere. Both have puzzled naturalists and sportsmen, and have awaited satisfactory answers. I too have had them in mind for many years, and have considered every available piece of tiger literature, particularly of the last century and even a little way before it, and travelled in the Sunderbans and outlying areas especially to see land and water configurations. I think now that there are answers for both.

There are many references to 'Royal Bengal Tiger' in Indian hunting accounts, and sportsmen have advanced theories for the name. Some have attributed the epithet 'Royal' as denoting the tiger's majestic appearance; others have described the ruff round the neck of some tigers as characterizing the 'Royal' tiger; and still others have put it down as a subspecies or variety of tigers of great size or great size of head. Another mark was said to be a mask of colour darker than the rest of the skin, running from the tip of the nose across the face to the base of the skull. Only the Sunderbans tigers were said to have the ruff and mark, and thus qualify to be called 'Royal'. There is also the suggestion that the appellation 'Royal' is appropriate because the tiger is 'king' of the Indian jungle.

However, a study of tiger-hunting continuously from the earliest days by the British after their advent in India throws light on the real origin of the name. It becomes clear that the epithets 'Royal' and 'Bengal' came into use only after the British arrival in India—a very significant point. There were no equivalents in the Indian languages used in the description of the tiger, either in eastern India or any other part of India, before then. They were wholly unknown.

Calcutta and Madras were the scenes of the first important British settlements. There was no tiger in the immediate hinterland of Madras, but there were tigers in plenty around the Calcutta of those days. Even as late as the 1880s, a tiger was shot by a superintendent of the Port Police inside the Botanical Gardens in Sibpur, now part of Greater Calcutta. Therefore, in British minds, the tiger came to be associated with Bengal— hence 'Bengal Tiger'.

The tigers which the British officers and adventurers hunted in the fifty or so miles around Calcutta, or the settlement which grew into Calcutta, later gradually extending their field of operations into the great swamps of the Sunderbans, were magnificent specimens. The colouring was striking, the climate and the thick steaming jungles contributing to its richness. These factors are now recognized as contributing to animal coloration. Moreover, in winter, when the British did most of their hunting, the tigers were better covered than at other times of the year, and consequently looked even more impressive, some animals growing ruffs round their necks. The winter months were cold, as is evident from the descriptions, and as they are sometimes even now despite immense vegetational and land changes from deforestation, river training, and marsh reclamation. So it was not long before the British, with their monarchical predilections, added 'Royal' to 'Bengal Tiger'. The terms come increasingly into use in later notes, and in books when books began to be written. For the benefit of readers other than British, a red deer of the Scottish Highlands with twelve or more points is called 'Royal Stag' in Britain, and is really no different from other stags except in the number of points in its antlers, the greater number naturally assuring a stag of impressive proportions, worthy of being the King's game. The 'Royal Tiger' carried the same significance.

Local incidents connected with British Royalty also contributed to establish the usage. One such related to the visit to India of the Prince of Wales (later King Edward VII) in 1875. In Purnea, now in Bihar State and closely adjoining West Bengal, after he had shot a tiger and praised the sport, the indigo planters, of whom Shillingford (one of the most important of the hunter-naturalists of that era) was the chief host, decided to add the prefix 'Royal' to 'Bengal Tiger'. Another famous hunter-writer of that period, Islington, has recorded this incident in his diary. Shillingford, as Chairman of the Planters' Association, decreed that it should be so.

And thus, by these several means, the 'Royal Bengal Tiger'

came into existence. It did not mean, nor was it intended to mean, that the tigers in Bengal, splendid specimens as they were, exceeded other tigers in size. The description gained substance as all hunting accounts were written by British sportsmen, and gradually became established in tiger lore. Habitat may cause differences in size and colour, but the investiture on these accounts with regal honours of the denizens of a particular range of forests in a country which was at that time overrun with tigers seems improbable.

Regarding the occurrence of the tiger in the Sunderbans, the popular, and only, theory so far is that tigers were carried down the flood waters of the two great rivers, the Ganga and the Brahmaputra, and their numerous tributaries, to their vast estuary in the Bay of Bengal, which the Sunderbans swamps represent. But there was no need for this to have happened at all. Geologists have told us of the comparatively recent origin of the Sunderbans, about two to three thousand years ago. Tigers which had penetrated into India from north Asia in prehistoric times lived in all parts of the sub-continent which offered suitable habitat, including the hot and humid jungles in the Gangetic plain. As the Sunderbans delta began to be formed, rapidly in geological time but slowly enough by human reckoning, with the changes in course of the Ganga-Brahmaputra system of rivers, the tiger extended its range farther south as more and more land was created and was covered by jungle. There was no factor inhibiting either the spread of the jungle or of the tiger in its wake. Other great animals extended their habitats too—the rhinoceros and the buffalo. The delta was wild and uninhabited, with an abundance of the tiger's natural prey and an equal abundance of thick cover in which to cool off in the heat of the day. All the tiger needed to do, in course of time, was to adapt itself to the gradually changing land and water conditions of more swampland and more brackish water, as ocean tides swept farther into the unstable land formations. It was an unconscious adaptation, and a slow one. The tiger was never entirely cut off from fresh water, as even now fresh water can be had in the Sunderbans in natural rain-water pans. It was this tiger that the British hunters encountered in all its wild majesty and soon named the 'Royal Bengal Tiger'. The sooner this description is discarded now, the better.

There is another kind of tiger which was much in the news in 1960–64. I refer to India's white tigers. The incidence of 'white' tiger in the jungles of the former Princely State of Rewa in central India, and occasionally in other dry, not too well-covered jungles in the same region has been recorded in sporting diaries from the mid-nineteenth century. From these accounts, it is not possible to know precisely whether there was partial or complete absence of pigment in individual specimens, as the common description of all pale-coloured tigers is 'white'. The Bombay Natural History Society is said to have recorded seventeen instances of 'white' tigers shot in the areas now covered by Madhya Pradesh, Bihar, Orissa, and Assam States in the period 1907–33. There does not seem to be a single authenticated case at any time of a 'white' tiger from outside Indian limits. The dispersion of the only known *family* of white tigers in animal history is therefore of considerable interest.

In Rewa alone, nine white tigers were shot in its former 13,000 square miles of forest, during the first half of this century, the last in 1947. Moth-eaten trophies remain in mute evidence; I have seen one or two but, with the passage of years, it is impossible to evaluate the original skin coloration, as no particular care has been taken for their preservation. The strange and fascinating history of the last of these tigers, now scattered in different parts of the world, began in May 1951.

A white cub was captured in a shoot—its mother and three other cubs, all normal-coloured, being killed—given the name of Mohan, and reared in captivity by the Maharajah, in the company of a normal-coloured female in the former fort-palace of Govindgarh. Its age at the time of capture was placed at nine months. Three litters were born to this pair, all normal-coloured. The tigress was then removed, and a female cub of the second litter, born in 1953 and named Radha, was given as mate to Mohan.

A first litter of four cubs to this pair was born in October 1958, one male and three females, and all were white. This was a unique event in tiger-breeding. A second litter was born in June 1960. This consisted of two white males and a normal-coloured female. A third litter of two white cubs, male and female, appeared in March 1962. A white female of Radha's first litter was now put with Mohan. In July 1963 two white cubs were born, but both died a few weeks later.

The white tigers were housed in the deserted fort-palace of the Maharajah at Govindgarh. It was a splendid establishment once, with innumerable rooms, and it is said that 1,500 guests could be accommodated in comfort at one time. But it had been abandoned, and its vast courtyards became overgrown with jungle. It provided what seemed an ideal home for the tigers, with plenty of space for them to roam about and in near-natural surroundings, and yet they could be kept under observation. So the entire family lived there, and it seemed a programme of controlled breeding was possible.

However, with his reduced resources after the end of the Princely States, the Maharajah sold a female of Radha's first litter, Mohini, to the Washington National Zoological Park in 1960. There, in course of time, she was mated with a normal-coloured tiger. Three cubs were born in 1964, only one white, the first white cub to be born outside India.

From the time of this sale, the fate of the remaining tigers began to be debated. The Maharajah wanted to sell more of the cubs to foreign zoos to pay for the upkeep of the Govindgarh *ménage*. Official attitude was opposed to the export of the rare beasts. The Maharajah was then left with two alternatives: to turn the tigers loose in Rewa's jungles, or put them in India's zoos if they would pay reasonable prices.

To set them at liberty had obvious dangers, and their survival in competition with wild tigers was at least problematic. For a while it seemed that, if export was not going to be allowed, this would become inevitable. However, after prolonged negotiations, the dispersion of nature's most princely family was agreed upon.

Two white tigers of the first litter of Mohan and Radha, a male and a female, named Raja and Rani, were bought by the Government-run Delhi Zoo. In 1966, three white cubs were born to this pair. Some time after, the parents were presented by the Prime Minister of India, Mrs. Indira Gandhi, to the French Government, who placed them in the Paris Zoo. Out of the two other white females of this litter, one had already gone to Washington. The other, Sukeshi, is still at Govindgarh, the mother of the last pair of white cubs to be born there, and also belongs to the Delhi Zoo.

In June 1963, the two white cubs of the third litter of Radha, a male and a female, Champa and Chameli, were sold to Bristol Zoo. One white cub was born to this pair in 1967 (died a few days after) and four more in 1968. In July 1963, the two white males of the second litter were acquired by the West Bengal Government for the Alipore Zoo in Calcutta, and named Himadri and Neeladri. This zoo also got in September 1963 the normal-coloured female of this litter, Malini, from the Delhi Zoo to which she had been sent, in exchange for another normal-coloured tigress. She was given as mate to Neeladri, and the result was the birth in July 1965 of two cubs, a white female and a normal-coloured male. Left at Govindgarh are Mohan, the original white tiger, and Sukeshi.

A carefully planned breeding programme in India might have led to the permanent establishment of the white strain. Now with the white tigers so widely dispersed, opportunities may be lacking to find suitable partners, at least from within the family. Tigers, and even more tiger cubs, sometimes die unexpectedly under zoo conditions. The jungles of Rewa are going too, and it is a matter for doubt if more white tigers will be found in them in future years.

Most people think of all white animals as albinos with a complete absence of skin pigment. The Rewa tigers are not albinos at all. They are an entrancing freak of nature by which the normal golden coat of the tiger has been turned to white or blue-white. The stripes are present as usual but tend to be ashy-grey instead of the usual black. They do not show up any more prominently than black stripes, the lighter-coloured stripes on the paler background cancelling the possibility of such an effect. The tigers are not pink-eyed albinos, but have blue eyes, the blondes of the tiger world.

Talking of the tiger's stripes, their pattern in each animal is distinctive, and individual animals can be easily recognized. I have used their facial markings for this purpose without difficulty.

Of true albino tigers, that is, tigers lacking all pigmentation, with pink eyes and no pigment in the iris, I believe there is only a single recorded instance. In 1927, in the former Princely State of Cooch Behar, now part of West Bengal, two three-quarter grown tigers of this description were reported shot. As almost

E

always, no scientific examination seems to have been made.

I have come across other accounts of sportsmen claiming to have seen white tigers in the Chanda and Hazaribagh jungles where conditions approximating to dryness and brilliant light are present. The last authenticated account appears to be the one given by the Rajasaheb Deo of Surguja in the *Journal of the Bengal Natural History Society* dated June–December 1959. He wrote of the shooting of a white tiger in the forests of the erstwhile Princely State of Surguja, now in Madhya Pradesh, and also referred to the first white tiger shot in that tract in 1922. A photograph of the slain tiger is printed alongside the account.

We once camped for a week in the Hazaribagh National Park, and the forest ranger at Rajderwa, within the Park, told me of the incidence of white tiger in the Park. He said he had seen one, more than once. I spent some days looking for it, following all tiger trails I picked up, but did not see any tiger at all. Once a tiger jumped right across the forest road in front of our cruising van, but I was in the back of the van and missed it. It was, however, a normal-coloured tiger.

What makes the white tigers additionally fascinating is the fact that colour variation among tigers in India has been a subject of endless speculation over a century. But the limited opportunities a single observer has of seeing the tiger in all its more important homes have prevented any conclusive answer. Description of colouring has a large personal factor attached to it, however reliable an individual observer may be. The tiger is an exclusively Asiatic animal, and the vast extent of its geographical distribution within historic times, south of a line stretching from the Sea of Okhotsk and the Amur river in the east, through Lake Baikal and the southern shores of the Aral and Caspian Seas to the river Euphrates, has also prevented close study and conclusive result.

But it may be said that high temperature, excessive humidity, and reduced light conditions encourage melanism, or excess of dark or black skin or hair pigmentation, whereas the opposite conditions of dryness and brilliant light may be said to have the effect of reducing colour tones and producing sandy-coloured animals. Accordingly, tigers in the hot and humid forests, as in the swamp-jungles of the Sunderbans, are generally known to be more darkly or vividly coloured than tigers in other parts, while those occurring in arid desert-like jungles such as those of central India have been seen to be light-coloured.

I have included in this book a picture of tiger carcasses laid out on trestles in a Naga village, and a picture of an ingenious wild tiger trap used by a Prince in his forest in pre-independence days. I will say a few words about each of these subjects as parts of the lore about the tiger on which nothing has been written.

Nagas in the extreme east of India, on the Sino-Burmese border, are renowned hunters, but of their hunting tigers little is known outside their territory. Tiger-hunting with the Nagas is not a sport. Tigers are hunted only when they attack village cattle or otherwise become a nuisance.

The offending tiger is located in a ravine, and driven, somewhat as in a beat, towards a V-shaped stockade erected at the bottom end of the ravine. When the tiger sees no way of escape in front—spearmen stationed behind the stockade posts drive it back if it charges the stockade—it tries to break back. The circle of hunters who have been following it now throw their spears. This may be repeated several times, till the tiger is badly wounded and exhausted. Then a gap in the circle is deliberately made to tempt the tiger to escape. This it tries to do, when the hunter nearest to it closes in with his *daoh*, or hunting dagger, and despatches it.

Tigers when slain are carried back to the village and set up on trestles, and there is a celebration that night. No part of the carcass is made any use of, and it is allowed to decay naturally. The picture is of August 1964, when wild life in the Brahmaputra valley in Assam was driven to higher ground following extensive flooding of the valley in the heavy monsoon rains, and these tigers apparently moved westward and entered Naga domains.

In the days of Princely India, the tiger was not only in demand for the world's zoos, but additionally for the private collections of the Princes or for being put into an arena for the animal fights that used to be staged for the onlookers' pleasure. Many ingenious devices were used to capture wild tigers, and the picture shows a trap which I have seen and is still in good preservation.

It is now inside the Hazaribagh National Park. It is a

twenty-foot deep pit with sides sloping slightly inward, and about thirty feet in diameter, with a masonry pillar three feet across at the top at its centre. This pillar supports the apex of a triangular platform of brushwood, the opposite end of which rests on the side of the pit. The platform was covered over with earth and grass to present a natural appearance. A live bait was tied on the pillar and attracted the tiger. If the tiger walked on to the platform, it collapsed under the tiger's weight. Or, if the tiger sprang across the platform to the pillar top, which had not space enough, the platform collapsed also. Either way, down went the platform to the bottom of the pit, carrying the tiger with it.

A tunnel leads from the pit bottom to the ground level above. The only avenue of escape for the tiger was this tunnel. It therefore rushed up the tunnel, but only to enter a two-compartmented steel-barred cage kept invitingly open at the tunnel mouth with a second bait tied in the rear half. No sooner had the tiger entered the cage than both the entry door and the door between the compartments crashed shut by means of a spring arrangement.

Another trap is in the Ramgarh forest, some miles from Jaipur. It is a rectangular tower-like brickwork structure about twenty feet high, with a $3\frac{1}{2}$-foot square opening on its front side. Over this slides a door with steel bars, which was operated from the top of the tower by thick ropes. The door and some shreds of rope are still there. The bait was tied inside the tower. Its bleats inveigled the tiger into entering the tower, when the steel door was promptly let down by men waiting on the tower. After a period of starvation, the tiger readily entered a steel cage brought to the opening, with a meal in it to entice him.

Jim Corbett feared in 1946 that the tiger would become extinct in the wild state in ten years from then. However, the tiger has survived, but its continued existence in that state for much longer cannot now be taken for granted. Gee estimated that the present population would be about 4,000, compared to an estimated 40,000 fifty years ago. There was no one more knowledgeable than Gee, but I believe his figure could be too high in this instance. My own figure is less than 3,000, around 2,800, arrived at after considering all forest blocks of the tiger's habitat, and not forgetting the saying among jungle people, 'For every tiger you see, at least five see you'.

This may, on first sight, appear too low a figure. But in many, many forests, tiger only exists, not in the flesh, but from former associations, and these associations can be very strong. Who would have thought, for example, even fifteen years ago, that the tiger would become virtually extinct in southern India by the present time? But the opening up of the forests and their overrunning by jeep-riding sportsmen from towns and project centres have transformed the scene. The various sanctuaries hold only a small percentage of the total number between them while, outside of them, it is going to be difficult to stop even legalized tiger-shooting, for not only is this a good foreign exchange earner, but also sportsmen (good ones) expect to be allowed their quota in pursuit of the traditional sport. I give my figure not to alarm, but merely as being near what I believe is the fact.

Cheetal reported a new menace to the tiger's survival in May 1968. A market was rapidly growing for tiger-skins, with foreign tourists the main buyers. An estimated total of one thousand skins were sold in New Delhi, the centre for the trade, during the winter of 1967–68, with skins fetching as much as Rs.5,000 each. The skins no doubt represented the harvests of many years. (Demand in the West for leopard pelts is tremendous, and leopards both in Africa and India have been slaughtered on a mass scale in recent years.)

Export of tiger-skins has now been totally banned by the Government of India.

III

THE FLIGHT OF THE ELEPHANTS

Nature's great masterpiece, an elephant
The only harmless great thing.

JOHN DONNE

NO ONE KNOWS to any degree of exactitude how many wild elephants there are left in India. Certainly they must run to a few thousand, perhaps six to seven. The Indian elephant (*Elephas maximus*) now occurs in the States of Uttar Pradesh, Bihar, Orissa, Bengal, Assam, and Nagaland in the north, and Madras, Mysore, and Kerala in the south.

Opinions on size vary, but the biggest probably reach ten feet at the shoulder, although occasionally they may even be larger. Height measurement of elephants after death is a hopelessly inaccurate affair; no allowance can be made for the slump of the great body as it lies sideward and forward, and no measurement can be taken at all when it lies collapsed on its legs and in a sitting position. But there is an easy and satisfactory way of assigning the height. It consists simply in measuring the circumference of one of the elephant's forefeet from a point on firm ground and multiplying it by two. Care must be taken in such a measurement on loose soil, when the pressure of the feet would have splayed the soil around and lead to an exaggerated figure. Care too must be taken to make the measurement only from footprints which are not overlaid by the oval prints of the hind legs, as they normally are when the elephant ambles along.

After all this, however, the height in itself is not necessarily an indication of the strength or power of an elephant; nor is the length of the tusks. A tusker with short tusks may be more powerful than another with long tusks. A tuskless bull, or *makna*, is often a tremendously strong animal, thick-set in body and trunk. There are many recorded instances of *maknas* worsting big tuskers in fighting in the wild.

It was in the Periyar Wild Life Sanctuary many years ago that I made my first acquaintance with wild elephants, and incidents from that trip still stand out in my elephant memories. This is one of the very few remaining areas with a promise of permanent refuge for the Indian elephant, and consequently one of the most important of Indian wild life sanctuaries.

The Periyar river, rising from the western slopes of the Anaimalai Hills ('*anai*' means elephant and '*malai*' means mountain, in both Tamil and Malayalam, the languages of the region), was dammed in 1897, and most of its waters which flowed to waste to the Arabian Sea in the west were turned to flow into the river Vaigai flowing east to the Bay of Bengal, through a 6,000-feet tunnel, and used to irrigate large areas which suffered permanently from drought. This project has been described as involving the 'most extraordinary feats of engineering ever performed by man', and by all accounts was a monumental engineering achievement against tremendous obstacles. The designer and chief constructor was Col. J. Pennycuick, R.E.

The artificial lake formed by the dam became bounded by the lusciously vegetated hills of the region, one of the most famous in India for its abundance and variety of wild life. The scenery is picturesque rather than spectacular. The lake is 12·5 square miles in area and fed by the copious rainfall on the western side of the mountain divide. By today's standards, it is a small irrigation project, but it is an object lesson in the saving of the surrounding areas from devastation, because out of them has grown the present sanctuary. Forty years after the building of the dam, the sanctuary was created round the lake at the instance of the then Maharajah of Travancore, the Princely State within which it was placed—a far-sighted action in view of the subsequent rapid extermination of wild life everywhere in those hills. Many stories are told of the efforts of the first Warden, an Englishman, to establish the sanctuary securely and to develop salt-licks where the congregating animals could be seen.

The sanctuary is reached by road from Kottayam, with its

scrubbed-and-swept look, characteristic of Kerala small towns and villages. Few drives can be pleasanter. The road runs over flat ground with paddy fields and clusters of coconut trees on both sides. Fresh winds and cool air tell the visitor that hilly country is ahead. As the road rises, it is soon hemmed in by tea, rubber, and pepper plantations, although these are by no means continuous. The visitor duly arrives at Peermade, where the Peermade Game Reserve is an extension of the sanctuary itself. The wild life here is looked after by the Peermade Game Association, founded long ago by British planters. The journey ends with one's arrival at Aranya Nivas, the excellent State hotel, which is within the sanctuary and overlooks the lake.

The lake is an extraordinary sheet of water. It looked eerie with blackened stumps sticking out of it everywhere, and my wife asked how on earth it was going to be possible to get about by boat, which is the only permitted means of movement in the sanctuary—that is, without special dispensation (I have got off the boat to follow and photograph elephants). An enthusiastic waterwoman, Diana announced that this was one lake in which she would not on any account steer the motor-driven launch —we found out later she would not have been allowed to in any case—which we could see was moored at the foot of the path descending from the hotel to the lakeside. An inquiry revealed that, after the dam was built, no attempt was made to cut down the trees in the hollows between hills, with the result that as the trees rotted away in the lake which was formed, their trunks remained in the water, presenting a hazard to navigation. However, as I was to know later, the Forest Department's boatmen were completely familiar with their location and arrangement, and had no problem in steering the launch through the labyrinth. As no boats other than those belonging to the sanctuary or the Peermade Game Association are allowed on the lake, no danger really exists.

The lake runs north and south for some seven miles, with long or short tongues of water running from the main sheet in every direction. Lush greenery starts almost from the water's edge. Lofty trees of every description cover the hills, festooned with giant creepers and undergrown with luxuriant bamboo. The densely forested ravines, or *sholas* as they are called in those parts, are the natural homes of the elephants. The sanctuary contains

14 The Periyar Sanctuary, with one of its motor-launches on the lake. Some tree stumps can be seen sticking out of the water

15 An elephant herd drinking at the lake, Periyar Sanctuary

16 Elephant herd in the Anaimalai Hills

17 The Jaldapara *musth* tusker. One *musth* hole can be clearly seen between his ear and eye

18 Tusker demonstrating at Krishnan, after a charge, from the other side of a *nullah*, Mudumalai Sanctuary

19　Rhino in wallow, Kaziranga Sanctuary
20　A cattle egret and two pied myna sitting atop a rhino, Kaziranga. They per-
　　form useful services to the rhino by picking ticks and parasites off the hide

21 Close-up of rhino with a good horn, Kaziranga. This is as close a picture of a rhino as has ever been taken in the wild, showing what a massive animal it is

22 Bull rhino with 12-inch horn, Kaziranga Sanctuary

23 Rhino cow and new-born calf, Mihimukh, Kaziranga Sanctuary. The calf disappeared the day after this photograph was taken, probably taken by a tiger

24 A pair of wild cheetahs in the Deccan jungles

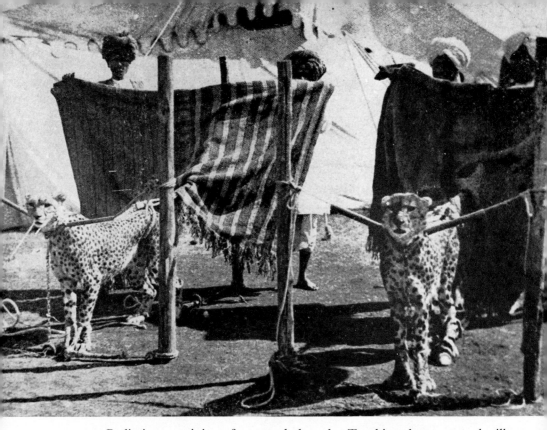

25 Preliminary training of captured cheetahs. Teaching them to stand still
26 Teaching a cheetah to hunt while still held in leash

a varied wild life, including the Nilgiri langur and the lion-tailed macaque, both of which monkeys are now threatened with extinction. They are killed by local people in all parts of their range in the Western Ghats for their flesh, and soup made from them is highly regarded as a rejuvenant. Earlier on that trip we had stopped one late evening at a local planter's house in the High Ranges. We were actually offered 'black monkey soup' (both monkeys are black in their bodies) instead of tea, with the guarantee that it would make us perk up. We may have looked tired, but we drank tea.

We made trips in the launch at the break of dawn or late in the evening. The cruises were usually made by clinging to the western shore of the lake on the outward journey, crossing over to the eastern side later, and returning along that shore, making sorties into those creeks and byways of water which seemed promising. The best of many trips was when we saw a small herd of elephants coming down to drink soon after dawn on the western shore. They were led by a tusker, a large beast but without big tusks. Cows and youngsters followed. As they reached the water, the bull held back ungallantly, and a cow stepped forward and stuck one of her forelegs in the water, clearly testing for depth and firmness of lake bed. First one foreleg, then another, was carefully lowered into the water and the ground prodded before she was satisfied all was well for the herd to enter the lake. Perhaps, more than depth, she was concerned about the firmness of the lake bed, as elephants are greatly scared of sucking mud and quicksands. Caught in one of these, the ponderous beasts have little chance of escape. One tiny calf which tried to rush past her into the water was uncere-moniously stopped by a swinging yank of her trunk, and skidded to a stop with much squealing.

Once they were all in the water, their joy was obvious. What a grand time they had! They plunged and dived, sometimes only the boss of the head or the high point of the back showing above the water. The tip of the trunk came up from time to time for air. They sucked up water in their trunks and squirted it over their backs or at one another. We were now quite close to them, no more than perhaps fifteen yards, and had been moving in by cutting off the motor and using short paddles. The boatmen did not approve of all this, knowing that elephants are powerful swimmers. However, the merry beasts took no notice. The frolicking went on for a quarter of an hour, before they began to step lazily out of the water, the calves still full of joy. The march back into the forest was accomplished with the bull covering the retreat.

On another occasion, as we were drifting in a *shola* creek, the air was suddenly rent by some shrill trumpeting. Moving quickly in the direction of the sound, we were delighted to see a young bull elephant gambolling on a knoll, now running down headlong into the water, now clambering out of it, running round and round, in the sheer joy, it seemed, of being alive. It was a primeval scene and full of pleasure. He kept this up for several minutes, taking not the slightest notice of us, before ambling off into thick jungle. Another time, we saw, from a good distance, a solitary tusker standing knee-deep in water. Slowly we approached, and he watched us but without alarm. As we drew near, he heaved himself out of the water, climbed on to the shore, stopped and turned for a good, long look, and sauntered away to less disturbed pastures.

The calm of these elephants showed that they, at least, were free from human persecution in the sanctuary, though we had heard that gaur, deer, and pig were being badly harassed by poachers. An incident on a hillside provided us with a point of interest in elephant herd behaviour. A bunch of elephants appeared round the hill and soon strung out single-file on the somewhat bare slope along what seemed a well-worn elephant path. As they moved, something seemed very wrong with one of the biggest of them, a bull with medium-sized tusks, who got left behind. He was limping badly and could scarcely put his right foreleg down. The rest of the herd did not wait, but walked well ahead of the straggler, till they stopped for a feed off some very green-looking bamboo clumps. The lame elephant came up with the herd in due course, and was soon lost to sight as he mingled with the others. After a while, the herd started moving forward again, and once more the same big elephant hobbled behind. This was still the position when they finally disappeared round the far hump of the hill. African big game hunters have given first-hand accounts of elephants assisting an injured or incapacitated comrade, even to the extent of raising him up from where he had fallen from gunshot and hustling him away from the scene of danger. In this case, none of the other elephants even paused once to assist their badly limping companion. But this elephant may have been suffering from a permanent injury or an injury which was taking a long time to heal. In nature, animal sympathy for one another, where it exists, cannot last over a long period of time, and the herd may have grown to accept the bull's injury as a handicap with which he and they had to live. The oft-repeated assertion that nature tolerates only able-bodied animals, and that maimed or incapacitated ones are killed off, is not true, but is a product of man's logic.

Once there was a splendid group of about ten elephants, bulls, cows, and calves, a couple of hundred yards from the shore, on rising ground. I persuaded the boatmen to put me down on the shore. They did, protestingly. The shore was full of fresh elephant footprints, which led directly up to the group. They had obviously played and drunk there, before starting on another gargantuan feed. I slowly crept up the grassy, tree-covered slope. I got as close to the elephants as I dared, but in a direct line with the boat for retreat in an emergency. But the morning light was so tricky and the vegetation so thick that photography was impossible. After watching for a while, I stole back to the boat, very much to the boatmen's relief.

The friend who was our host and guide on this Kerala trip of ours told us an extraordinary elephant story. He is a rubber planter, and had personally verified the story after the incident had taken place. Workers in a plantation adjoining the sanctuary had been roused one midnight by loud and repeated elephant trumpeting. None ventured to investigate until after dawn, when a group of them proceeded towards the scene of the disturbance. They saw a cow elephant wedged in between two stout trees and unable to extricate herself. A huge bull was standing by, and was repeatedly and vigorously trying to force her out. It was obvious that mating had taken place, and the cow had taken up her position to bear the bull who was an exceedingly large beast. After the mating, she had been so forced between the two trees that she was unable to pull herself out of the vice-like grip. The workers dared not go near, and the bull resented any move forward by them. Soon a crowd gathered, but the bull made no attempt to interfere with them as long as they remained where they were. He stayed with the cow the whole day, struggling to release her, till the poor cow seemed to be in great pain. As night fell, the men returned to their lines. The trumpetings ceased that night. The morning after, the men found the cow dead, and the bull gone. It seemed the bull had made off after realizing the hopelessness of his efforts to extricate his mate, and the cow had then given up the fight and died. It was a tragic and unusual story.

In July 1959 the Game Warden we had met in Periyar was killed in the Peermade Game Reserve by a wild elephant. The tragedy occurred when he and some *shikaris* were pursuing a tusker, who had been causing extensive damage to plantations outside the reserve. According to the report of the incident, one of the *shikaris* fired at the elephant but succeeded only in wounding it. The infuriated animal chased the party, and all escaped but the Game Warden, who was caught and trampled to death. How the Game Warden with all his knowledge of wild elephants embarked on a hunt for an animal known to be dangerous with so many others and, having done so, why he permitted one of them to shoot before he did was not stated.

Another important home for the Indian elephant is the Bandipur Wild Life Sanctuary in the State of Mysore. It is the inner sanctum of twenty square miles of the Venugopal Wild Life Park of 310 square miles which was established by the Maharajah of Mysore in 1941. Today, it is one of the most important refuges for wild life in the country as it is contiguous with the Mudumalai Wild Life Sanctuary in the neighbouring State of Madras. I went to Bandipur for the dual purpose of seeing and filming elephant and gaur, and of finding out if any tigers were left in the tract.

I arrived at Bandipur camp from Bangalore after a long but pleasant drive on asphalted or concrete road. In the succeeding days I made my best-ever films of elephant in the mixed forests of trees, bamboo, and tall grass. The bamboo at the time of my visit was dried and dead, and another bamboo cycle had come to an end. From the ashes of the dead bamboo would grow a fresh crop, and this endless regeneration will go on till, one day, the project men arrive with their bulldozers and their sales talk. The rains had just begun, the forest looked fresh, and the trees dripped moisture. Some places were dense with intertwining foliage and fern, and elsewhere the forest was without any undergrowth that could impede.

My first elephant was a beautiful tusker, and he was feeding, splendidly monarchical, close by the forest road on which my companion, forest ranger Mayappa, and I were walking briskly along. It was a perfect setting for the great beast, with the outline of mountains, blue and afar, for a backdrop, and the green leaves of the trees contrasting yet complementing the red moist earth to perfection. It was a poignant and timeless scene. The whirr of my filming disturbed him but slightly, and we looked at each other, I liked to think with friendly interest. He fed on for a while, and when he finally walked away, it was without a trace of agitation. While one would not call this location as being right off the beaten track, wild animals encountered in far-away places are quite unafraid of humans. Consequently, there is no need for the humans to be unduly afraid of them. Let them be, and they let you be. This is not too much of a generalization, as it has been my repeated experience. I have approached close to many so-called dangerous beasts, oft-times on foot, and they have been curious but in no way aggressive, stared at me with an ingenuous simplicity, but not pressed the acquaintance. In areas where they have been pursued or persecuted, it is an altogether different matter, and the greatest caution is necessary.

There was a group of three elephants across a grassy and undergrown bank of a *nullah*, and we approached them downwind. As the great blue-grey animals spread out on the far side, they made a magnificent picture in the late evening with the massed woods behind them, but letting the light shafts of the sun through, the sky beginning to change its hue of iris-blue to one of nasturtium-orange, and the cool breeze wafting to us the scents of the watercourse and the wild flowers that grew on its moist banks. We followed them down the gentle slope to the *nullah*, without being seen or scented as the wind was now blowing well our way, and the great beasts browsed and fed, now drawing close together, now drawing apart, till they disappeared in the long grass which in the far side woods grew under the trees.

There was the large tusker across the moss-scummed patch of water, feeding in typical elephant-lazy fashion on a grassy slope. The angle of the slope was perilously steep, and it seemed he might slip at any moment, slide, and tumble into the green slime. My side of the pool was steep and slippery too, and as I edged forward holding on to trunks of trees, I marvelled at the balance of the unconcerned leviathan, who seemed to be able to walk forward or back or sideways with an enviable sure-footedness.

We had some excitement with two elephants in a heavily undergrown patch of forest, with waist-high grass and dotted with trees. One of them was a large bull, very curious, and he scented us and came slowly forward. We kept very still, and after a good, long stare he went back to the business of feeding. When it seemed he had forgotten our existence, we moved forward, but he was keeping half a proboscis trained on us, for he took a few steps towards us again, with upraised trunk. We were pretty close to him, but I do not think he was aggressively inclined. But when the grass became higher and we could only see him from the gleam of his tusks, it was time to depart and leave him in peace.

There was, too, another tusker who decided to have an even closer look at us. We first saw him in a distant tree clump. It seemed he soon scented us, for he came swishing in the long grass past the trees at a swinging pace, which began to put thoughts of a lightning getaway in our minds, till, at the very edge of the grass, he stopped and lifted his trunk high to smell the tainted air. Elephants are notoriously short-sighted, and rely almost entirely on scent and hearing for protection. They detect, of course, movement at near range. This elephant was a giant, with long tusks which gleamed in the evening sun. We stood perfectly still on the forest path, a breathless pause which lingered and grew. We were tensed at his gently swaying trunk, and there were only a few yards of clearing between him and us. The van in which we had entered the forest was parked a long way away. After what did not exceed perhaps a couple of minutes, the elephant seemed to move forward slightly, but still his vast bulk below the head was hidden. We held our ground and, as long as we did not panic, were reasonably safe. Elephants have not been hunted in this forest for a long time, and they had no reason to be aggressive. (If the elephants persecuted across the border in Madras State begin to arrive here, as it looks as if they might, then it will be a different story.) Our tusker now decided that enough was enough, turned, and walked away in the grass parallel to the path.

Elephant had been difficult to approach in the Corbett National Park, and elsewhere in the Kumaon Hills, and although I have wandered far and wide in this tract on a number of occasions, I saw them only in the Park. Once, with my wife and sons, we were moving about the bed of the Ramganga river on two riding elephants when we came upon two mother elephants, each with a calf. A little later, a third mother appeared, also with a calf. It was quite a pretty little party! We stayed still where we were, watching them. Mothers accompanied by their calves become restless if disturbed, and two of the cows began to show unmistakable signs of unease as the minutes passed. I thought it prudent to retire. Elsewhere, in north-western Uttar Pradesh, elephants have been something of a problem in the last few years, following the great deforestation that has been taking place. This has driven the elephants into the interior of the foothill jungles, whence they sometimes sally out to their former feeding grounds and cause considerable alarm and damage.

The most recent large-scale incursions by these elephants occurred in mid-1964. The newspapers treated the public to 'rampaging elephants' and 'elephant devastation' and many other superlative descriptions calculated to foster public awakening to conservation of wild life. In India, newspapers similarly excel themselves when man-eating tigers are active, in Orissa or Uttar Pradesh or elsewhere, by headlines such as 'Bloodthirsty tigers on the prowl', 'Striped terrors stalk the country' (these are taken from actual accounts), and other apt descriptions. This is symptomatic of their approach to wild life. Needless to say, the reports were often wildly exaggerated.

It was true, however, that the elephants did suddenly appear outside the forests where it was safer for the people of the region that they should remain. It seemed a kind of spontaneous eruption, because an area of approximately two thousand square miles was concerned. The primary affected area was the Dun valley, and exaggerated reports of people killed began to be circulated. Men were said to be living in fear of their lives and to scurry to their homes and wait in terror behind barred doors.

The elephants were primarily concentrating on eating the sugarcane from the cane plantations which are extensive in that part of Uttar Pradesh, and also helping themselves to feeds from planted bamboo forests. They had crossed the river Ganga in strength, and had caused considerable damage to young *sal* plantations, trampled cultivated fields, and knocked down outposts and huts in their triumphal onward march. The damage was estimated to run into *lakhs*[1] of rupees. And, as a crowning humiliation, they knocked down the boundary walls of the new antibiotics plant in Rishikesh, set squarely in the middle of one of their former migration routes. The Uttar Pradesh Government acted with promptitude. They withdrew the protection given to wild elephants under their 85-year-old Wild Elephants Protection Act, and announced a reward of Rs. 200 to *shikaris* for each wild elephant killed, with a present of the beast's ivory in addition. It was also notified that the Forest Department would plan extensive *kheddah*[2] operations, which had been discontinued everywhere in India as elephants were no longer in demand for forestry operations, and of course not for Princely elephant stables. The few animals for supply to zoos and circuses could be had from the offspring of domesticated cows.

It was worthwhile finding out what it was that had prompted this aggressive march, for wild elephants left to themselves in their natural homes are peaceful beasts, and give no trouble to man or any other animal. The case against them was that they had invaded areas of human occupation and laid them waste, and consequently posed a threat to the people of the area. But the truth was quite the opposite of this, and something had previously happened which had created the situation. It was a simple cause-and-effect relation. The Siwaliks, the Dun valley, and the great submontane forests on the north-western parts of Uttar Pradesh had been their immemorial home, certainly one of the most important for the Indian elephant from before the dawn of history. In certain seasons, they descended from the hills to the valleys, by way of certain well-defined migration routes from the Siwaliks, across the Ganga river, and to the

[1] *Lakh* = 100,000.

[2] Elephant-catching in a stockade.

Dun valley. Without the smallest thought being given to the conservation of their habitat and ancient migration routes, the forests have been felled, land cut and seared, watercourses altered and new ones created, and, indeed, the land scene transformed beyond recognition. The vast majority of the elephants retreated in the face of this intense persecution, and those that did not were trapped or killed. The ones that retired made some kind of an adaptation to circumstances. As a whole, the elephant population fell considerably, inevitably in such a situation. No reliable data are available for numbers, but the sometimes-expressed theory that elephants have increased can be discounted. It is not possible that this could have happened when all the factors were hostile to such increase. Reduction would follow a reduction in natural foodstuffs through a decrease in longevity and reproductive rate and an increase in disease. Nothing more than superficial reliance can be placed on official estimates, and I would rely more on the knowledgeable local residents with whom I talked when I visited the area some months later. They were of the view, with few exceptions, that there were fewer elephants now than a quarter of a century ago, that the danger and damage from the 1964 incidents had been exaggerated, and that the methods used to tackle the elephants were inefficient and cruel.

Habitat destruction was particularly severe in the years after the last war. Some of it was inevitable with expanding human needs, but had some thought been given to stabilizing the elephant population in the tract, forests with natural food supply could have been selected for conservation, migratory routes protected, and human expansion directed towards areas not quite so important to the elephants. But tract after tract of forest went under the axe. When the dormant migratory urge came upon the harassed beasts, they were quite helpless to forgo the primeval urge, held in check for so long by environmental factors. They poured down into the valley, with what results has been seen. A discussion of the unplanned and wasteful exploitation of the forests and of the causes which led to the elephant invasion may appear pointless and of no practical use. This is really not so, because there are still undeveloped areas left where, if the principles of conservation are applied, nature and wild life can be saved without dishonour and given a

F

chance to survive, and at the same time the long-range interests of the people can be protected.

The means advocated to check the elephants-at-large were as incompetent as they were cruel. The raiding animals were un-injured to begin with, and it was well worth while to try and drive them back to their forests. This is not as dubious a measure as it may seem on first sight, because wild elephants can some-what easily be driven by noise alone. They quickly get frightened and can be moved in any desired direction. Such a drive is of course a skilled operation and has to be carefully organized and led. If, however, a certain amount of shooting became in-evitable, there should have been no doubt that it should have been undertaken by the Forest Department, or entrusted to experienced elephant hunters; or, if there were none of this category, for elephant has not been hunted in India for a long time, to hunters with wide experience of big game shooting. It was wholly wrong to leave it to *shikaris*, most of whom cannot even kill deer and pig cleanly. I was told, later, that they did leave wounded elephants, which no doubt turned rogue. All wild life suffers badly if left wounded, but elephants even more than others, as they do not die from wounds which would kill other animals in the course of some days, but live on, the wounds festering and often extending. A serious elephant wound may take months or even years to heal; in the meantime, the poor beast suffers intensely. Elephants, both wild and captive, associate man-inflicted injuries with man, and distrust humanity as a consequence. There are many recorded instances of camp and zoo elephants which have shown active dislike for particular men, always with good cause.

The raiding herd in the Dun valley was not necessarily aggressive. With the migratory urge upon them, and bewildered by the disappearance of feeding grounds on their traditional route, the beasts had no alternative but to raid sugarcane and bamboo plantations to subsist while on the move. This kind of excitement in a herd soon disappears, and even left to themselves they would in the normal course have returned to their homes in the hill forests. A dangerous situation had been created entirely by human agency, and there was no short-cut way of bringing it back to the situation that existed before the invasion.

No particular watch seems to have been kept on the march-route of the elephants, when it might have been possible to tell if they were veering back to their forests. On the other hand, a premature lead was given to their killing and wounding, adding certain danger to the confusion.

When elephants embark on long marches such as these, they do so for fresh forage and water, and follow precisely the same routes. It has been observed in East Africa, and other parts of Africa too, that herds follow these routes within yards time after time, and in areas under enlightened control well-defined alleys have been left clear for the passage of the elephants. Indian elephants have now been for many decades restricted to comparatively small expanses of forest, and to a large extent have been forced out of their migratory habits. But where such migration still occurs, it is excessively cruel to eliminate it by offering monetary rewards for their killing. If any lesson has been learnt from the 1964 experience, the needs of the elephants can be taken into account and provision made for them. The elephant is quite capable of making a good deal of adaptation. An example can be given from the Kaziranga Wild Life Sanctuary in Assam, where in recent years elephants have taken to including the water-hyacinth plant in their diet. This plant was not present there but, from what reason is not known, has now taken root and spread so enormously that great patches of swamp are entirely covered by it.

There are now probably no more than 700 to 800 elephants in north-western Uttar Pradesh, out of an estimated 1,000 animals in all of that State. There is still enough forest area to support them, and provided their management is handled intelligently, their intrusions into populated areas can be checked. But elephants make news only when they become destructive. When a pair of them descended on the telephone exchange in Kashipur, in the same area, one day in 1966, and wrecked it, the cry went up once again for their destruction.

Elephants are accused of being wasteful and destructive feeders. An adult elephant needs around 700 pounds of green fodder daily—an enormous amount. Furthermore, elephants are choosey in what they eat, by which I mean that they do not just fill themselves up with grass or leaves that are handy. Therefore, they certainly consume huge amounts of vegetation. But they are not such wasteful beasts as they are made out to be.

After all, before human interference with their feeding areas, there is no record of forests being destroyed by elephants beyond natural regeneration. Clumps of bush or trees may be pulled down to get at the juicy bits, but such vegetation recovers remarkably quickly in the natural course so that there is no permanent damage. Moreover, the shrubs and trees pulled down are not entirely wasted; other herbivores find food in them.

Wasteful trampling of vegetation does occur, but only when the elephants get into an excited state from fear, almost always man-inspired. Deep in the jungle, however, it is possible to arrive at a place which they have just vacated, and not notice immediately that a herd has been feeding there. To the trained eye, their passage is of course visible, but considering their tremendous needs, one cannot but be impressed with the quiet and economical feeding that has taken place. There is little unnecessary trampling down or uprooting of trees not directly connected with feeding. I have seen this too many times to believe anything different.

Elephant feeding in the undisturbed wild is a deliberate and methodical affair. There is none of the bolting down of food of the predators. If it is grass they are eating, a bundle of it is gathered in a winding movement of the trunk, and tapped with deliberation against the front legs to shake off the earth clinging to it. The bundle is then placed crosswise in the mouth and bitten through. The roots and the tops fall off, and the juicy middle portion is masticated and swallowed. Or, if it is fruit, flowers, or buds off the top of a tree they are after, the tree is slowly toppled by pressure from the forehead. Then the titbits are carefully picked up and put into the mouth. Or, if the bark of a favoured tree is the object, it is first split by applying the forehead once again, but not with so much pressure as would uproot the tree. Then it is taken hold of by the trunk and peeled off in flicks and jerks in long strips. To anyone sufficiently interested, watching a wild elephant feed can be an absorbing occupation.

My only experience with a wild *musth* elephant was in the Jaldapara Wild Life Sanctuary in north Bengal. This sanctuary near the Indo-Bhutan border is best known as the only refuge of any import for the great onehorned rhinoceros outside

Assam and Nepal. It comprises thirty-six square miles of riverain jungle over abandoned courses of a number of Himalayan rivers and streams, overgrown with tall grass and reeds and sprinkled with low-lying swamps. We as a family had had plenty of excitement there with rhino on a previous visit, but my last one in 1965 was marked by the encounter with the *musth* tusker.

There had been talk of this tusker in the camp, as he was reported to be in the vicinity. He had killed the largest riding elephant, a big tusker, a few months previously, and was even attributed with a man-kill or two, though I did not think this was true as he had not been proscribed. The camp tusker was attacked at night, when hobbled in the stable, and killed by a swift thrust of the raider's tusks into his brain. The attacker was driven away by shots fired in the air. He had been making a nuisance of himself for some time, visiting the camp for the cows. A short time before the fatal attack, he had been knocked down by the camp tusker in an unexpected meeting in the jungle, and it seemed he had paid off the score in deliberation, picking his adversary when hobbled and unprepared.

The wild tusker was now said to be in *musth*, in addition, and had once again taken to visiting the camp for the females. He had been frightened away on successive nights by the concerted shouting of the *mahouts*, or elephant drivers. Gee and Krishnan, who seemed to be the only non-professionals besides me attending the Symposium on Wild Life Conservation that was being held there—all the others were forest officers or retired forest officers—had seen him in the morning. I had arrived late, and so it was with high expectations that I went in the afternoon in his search with Krishnan, Gupta, a former Chief Conservator of Forests of West Bengal and a very knowledgeable and pleasurable companion, and Bhaduri, Professor of Zoology in the Calcutta University and a person of great charm. We were mounted on two elephants.

We entered the sanctuary by descending to the bed of the river Torsa, the chief river which flows through it. Crossing the first arm of the river, we entered a large sandy island dotted with reed and grass. No sooner had we done so than we saw the tusker in a tall clump, feeding peacefully. We were not far away, and he saw us almost simultaneously. Making a detour, we manoeuvred to get the sun behind us for photography, and light conditions were just about perfect for filming. He followed our movements by turning round himself to keep facing us, and as we stopped, filmed, and moved on, he stopped too and followed, his inwardly curving tusks showing up brilliantly in the evening sun. The tusks were sharp and looked about three feet long. He was a massive, thick-set beast, and looked around nine feet in height. The *musth* condition was perfectly visible and the fluid was pouring down both cheeks. In the next fifteen minutes, I received my best lesson in natural history from Krishnan. Although we were only about twenty-five yards away, he urged me to go on filming, predicting every move of the subject, instructing the *mahouts* to position our elephants to the best advantage, his own elephant keeping in the background, mine placed in a forward position for picture-taking. Having taken pictures of the wild tusker in the morning, he was now subordinating his interests to mine.

Our elephants then crossed the last arm of the river before the thick jungle of the sanctuary, and Krishnan brought the wild bull to the water's edge opposite to us, still at about twenty-five yards. The *musth*-befuddled beast performed in the next few minutes precisely as Krishnan's whispered commentary predicted. He threw dust over his back, rested his trunk on his tusks, raised it and waved it about, stepped into the water, now this leg, now the other, as if he was acting to direction. Watching him was one of my most fascinating experiences in the Indian jungle. When I had done with filming, we started down the forest glade behind us, an old fireline, and the tusker began to follow, once again in the manner and at the distance now being predicted by Krishnan. This procession lasted a few minutes, when we urged our elephants on, and turned into long grass, as it was best now to lose the wild elephant.

Musth in elephants is still an unexplained thing. There seems to be no other parallel in the animal kingdom. It occurs generally in adult males, both wild and captive, but there are authenticated, though rare, instances of cows in *musth*. The beasts get excitable, but not necessarily aggressive, unless external factors irritate them unduly during this period, which seems to be one of some affliction. There is no particular time of the year for the onset of *musth*. Whether the condition has sexual motivation is not known. But it is nothing like a rut.

The duration varies from a few days to a few weeks, and is not the same in successive 'attacks' in the same animal.

The physical signs of the approach of *musth* can be easily recognized. The region of the temples becomes swollen and looks tender. Soon, a thickish black or dark brown fluid oozes out of an orifice on either side of the face, between eye and ear, and runs slowly down the cheeks. Tame elephants in this condition sometimes become suddenly dangerous, possibly because they are not able to alleviate their distress as they seem to be able to do in the wild, and many have been known to kill their *mahouts* of many years with whom they have lived contentedly, and sometimes on terms of affection. Watchful *mahouts* forestall danger at the first signs, chain and hobble them, reduce the number and size of feeds, and mix soporifics with the feeds.

In the wild, *musth* elephants are not violent towards their kind, nor do they wander off to solitude. They remain with the herd, occasionally seeking relief by submerging in water or wallowing in mud. I have not come across any account of a *musth* elephant attacking his herd members, who apparently know to leave him well alone. The violence, therefore, of captive elephants in a similar state has probably something to do with their lack of freedom to do as they please. In short, far too little is known about *musth* in elephants for an objective appraisal to be made.

The Indian elephant faces an uncertain future. A great part of the plains forests have been felled, and operations have extended to the hill forests favoured by the elephant, where these have not been already lost through the great power and irrigation projects. Added to all this, there has been extensive and wanton slaughter in the remoter parts of Assam, such as in the Mizo Hills district. I have collected reliable reports of this slaughter, which describe the killing of elephants on a commercial scale by the Lushai tribes, who eat elephant meat and sell it in tribal markets in dried form. A returned traveller told me that he saw in many villages elephant trunks being dried in the sun. This has closely followed the almost total destruction of wild animal and bird life in the Naga territory, which the authorities chose to overlook for political reasons. The Lushais are said to have almost exterminated the wild elephants in their area, and then moved into the reserve forests of Cachar, such as the Lalcharra reserve forest, where they kill and wound the animals and return to their own territory. Elephants of both sexes and all sizes have been butchered or grievously wounded. Hunting has been facilitated by the destruction of heavy forest, authorized and unauthorized, leaving behind denuded areas guaranteed to make the elephants restless and migratory. Tea plantations in areas where there has been no trouble from elephants complain of raiding elephants, which enter the plantations in search of foliage, and of rogues, turned to this classification from wounds, attacking people. However, none of this has received anything but superficial official notice, the only action taken being to proscribe the rogues. In the far south also, another famous elephant area, the bamboo forests of Kakkankote, in the State of Mysore, will soon be a mere memory. These were the forests of the *kheddah* operations of G. P. Sanderson, described in his famous work *Thirteen Years Among the Wild Beasts of India* (1879), and will be submerged on the completion of the Kabini river hydro and irrigation project.

Sometimes reports emerge simultaneously from authorized sources, on the future of the elephants and official intentions about them, which are contradictory and must puzzle everyone not acquainted with the inside machinery of these sources. For example, a few years ago, one announcement said that there was serious official concern about the increase in the export of elephants abroad (I doubt if there was any such increase of significance), which it was considered would seriously affect India's elephant population. Simultaneously, another announcement called attention to the menace from the increasing numbers of wild elephants in the north-western forest divisions of Uttar Pradesh, and gave out the decision to resume elephant-catching for export! One other suggestion, quite seriously made, was to put captured elephants to work by making them drag ploughs on farms! It read:

Meanwhile more favourable results have been reported on the possibility of using elephants on farms. A new harness manufactured by the agricultural engineering workshop at Bareilly was tried out by forest officials at Lalkuan a few days ago. The elephants were able to hold board ploughs, but it seems that they would be able to manipulate disc ploughs better. It now appears that they would be useless for breaking up new lands, but they may prove suitable for follow-up operations. The Lalkuan tests were inconclusive and new trials will be shortly undertaken. Ordinary farmers in the *terai* area seem to have evinced little interest in the experiment. Even if elephants can be used, it would have to be shown how far the proposition is economically sound. Besides, the elephants' own pronounced sense of dignity has to be taken into account. Elephants do not like drudgery. They like work which involves some exercise of their intelligence and sense of order, as in timber operations. *Terai* colonizers have bitter experience of the proverbial elephants' revenge. Two *chowkidars*, who recently broke the code, had their homes searched out by a herd and were trampled to death.

A more fatuous statement on elephants is difficult to come by.

Elephants, like tigers, will continue to be credited with viciousness as long as their natural food supply is destroyed and in consequence they are forced to enter man's domains in search of food. Rogue elephants will be made out of peaceable beasts as long as amendments are made to game laws such as the one in the State of Madras a few years ago, which vested discretion with the District Collector 'to grant a licence to shoot wild male or female elephants for the protection of crops and plantations' from destruction on being satisfied of the urgent need for the issue of such a licence. Present-day District Collectors live far away from nature. To most of them any wild life automatically represents grave danger, the 'wild' not implying 'not domesticated' but 'dangerous'. With what ease this game law amendment can be turned to the benefit of someone wanting to shoot an elephant needs no discussion. Elephant! elephant! in my fields, and lo! the licence is at your elbow.

The ultimate survival of the Indian elephant in the wild state will depend on the attempts made to understand its ways and its needs. It is a sagacious beast, and will not be eliminated without putting up a struggle.

IV
THE LAST OF THE RHINOS

Nature alone knows what she aims at.
                    JOHANN WOLFGANG VON GOETHE

IT WAS around the year 1910 that concern seems to have been
first expressed about the future of the giant rhinoceros of Asia,
the great onehorned rhino (*Rhinoceros unicornis*). The then estimate of just over a thousand animals was sufficient cause for
alarm. The first steps to legislate for its protection in India were
initiated. Rhino were officially closed to sportsmen in Bengal
and Assam. Many years later, in 1932, the Bengal Rhinoceros
Act was passed, and in 1954 the Assam Rhinoceros Bill became
law. The bills prohibited the killing, injuring, or capture of any
rhinoceroses, and penalized contravention by fine or im-
prisonment.

Yet, this largest of the Asiatic rhinoceroses had a former range
extending from the north-western passes of India eastward
towards Burma, precisely how far east is not known. Historical
and hunting references leave no room for doubt that it must have
lived in large numbers once. Lydekker said in his *The Great and
Small Game of India, Burma, & Tibet* (1900):

> In the history of Timur-bec it is described how in 1398 on the
> frontier of Kashmir, Timur hunted and killed many rhino-
> ceros. In the memoirs of Baber it is described how in about
> 1519 he hunted rhinoceros in bush country near the Indus.
> And in the book of Sidi Ali dated 1554 it is stated that
> rhinos were seen near the Kotal Pass west of Peshawur.

The Emperor Babar wrote:

> Crossing the Black Water near Bigrain[1] we formed a hunting

[1]Peshawar.

ring, facing downstream. Presently someone came up with word that a rhino was in a small jungle near at hand, and riders had surrounded the jungle, waiting there for us. We rode on with a loose rein, spreading out to join the ring and raising an outcry. The shouting brought the rhino into the open. Humayun and those who had come across the mountains with him had never seen such a beast before, and were much amused. They followed it about two miles, shooting many arrows. It was brought down finally without having made a good set at a man or horse. Two others were killed.

I had often wondered how a rhinoceros and an elephant would behave if brought face to face. In this hunt the mahouts brought forward the elephants. One of the rhinos charged out where the elephants were. When a mahout put one of the elephants forward, the rhino would not stay but charged off another way.

Lydekker wrote further:

There is historical evidence to prove that during the early part of the sixteenth century the Indian rhinoceros was common in the Punjab, where it extended across the Indus as far as Peshawur; and down to the middle of the present century, or even later, it was to be met with along the foot of the Himalayar as far west as Rohilcund and Nepal, and it survived longer still in the Terai-lands of Sikkim. Not improbably, too, the rhinoceros found till about the year 1850 in the grass-jungles of the Rajmahal Hills, in Bengal, belonged to the present species.

It was about the time of Babar's hunt, in 1515, that the first Indian rhino is known to have been sent to Europe. It was a present from the King of Cambay to King Emmanuel of Portugal, and was shipped from Goa to Lisbon. A fight was arranged in Lisbon between this rhino and an elephant, and the elephant, upon seeing the rhino, is said to have burst the arena and fled! King Emmanuel, who must have been very impressed, then decided to present the rhino to Pope Leo X. It was shipped again, but the ship was caught in a storm in the Gulf of Genoa and sank with all hands and the rhino. This was the animal immortalized by Albrecht Dürer in an engraving; Dürer never saw the rhino but did his work from a sketch by a Portuguese artist.

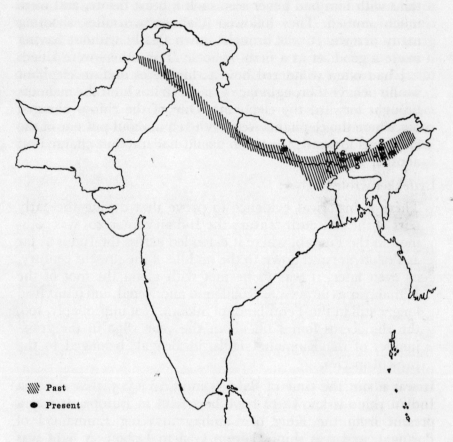

Past
Present

MAP I

Past and present distribution of the great onehorned rhinoceros. Survival areas are; 1 Kaziranga; 2 Sonairupa; 3 Orang; 4 Laokhowa; 5 Manas; 6 Jaldapara—Gorumara; 7 Chitawan (Nepal)

The first Indian rhino to enter England, in 1684, was paraded round the country for the next two years. But African rhinos had often been brought to Rome in classical times, probably the white or squarelipped rhinoceros, a more tractable animal than the black rhino.

In northern Bengal, the rhino was once sufficiently numerous to be saddled with a major responsibility for the destruction of rice and corn fields—with little justification, however, as the great Indian rhino is not a crop-destroyer, although occasionally it may enter cultivated fields for titbits. The government even offered a reward of Rs. 20 per head for its destruction.

In his *Thirty-seven Years of Big Game Shooting in Cooch Behar, the Duars, and Assam* (1908), the Maharajah of Cooch Behar records monotonously the slaughter of rhino (and other animals) in the Princely shoots he organized every cold weather and, indeed, it seems, at every opportunity. The 'best' sport seems to have been on a day in 1886. He writes, 'A blank day on the 15th was followed by a magnificent day's sport with Rhino near Rossik Bheel and Chengtimari or rather half a day's, for we bagged five rhinos before luncheon. I do not think this record has been beaten.' Today, from this once-plentiful rhino tract, the great beast survives only in the Jaldapara Sanctuary, with a few stragglers outside, estimated at about fifty-five animals in all.

How quickly can animals go! In a letter dated 31 May 1952, to *The Statesman*, Calcutta, Mrs. Jamal Ara, the noted Bihar naturalist, pleaded for a rhino sanctuary in Bihar. Rhinos in Bihar! It is already a thing of the past now. They were once plentiful there, below the Himalayan foothills and even some way into the interior, but Mrs. Ara was referring to survivors in the Purnea district. The last of these were killed off when work commenced on the huge Kosi river project in that area.

The position in India after the first world war was that sportsmen could not legitimately hunt the rhino. But, in Nepal—the second survival home of this rhino—it was a different story. The Cooch Behar record was no record there, and the former rulers' shoots used to lay low rhino by the score. High-caste Hindus and Gurkhas considered the flesh and blood highly acceptable to the gods. Those who could hunted the animal and offered libation of its blood after entering the disembowelled body. Special shoots arranged for distinguished visitors took heavy toll. Reading accounts of them, there seems to have been little real sport. The sportsmen were mounted on an army of trained elephants, the rhinos were surrounded, and then made large and slow-moving targets into which lead was pumped. The real thrill, one imagines, must have come later—in the photographs that were taken with the sportsman resting his right foot on the chopped-off head of the victim, with more heads lying about in the gore with their unevenly hacked necks. The photos advertised the hunter's skill and prowess to faraway relations and admirers. Far superior in the numbers of animals killed to anything in Bengal, a bag of ten or fifteen rhinos in a day at a specially convened shoot was nothing out of the ordinary.

The attitude of the highest in the land is typified in the following account given by Armand Denis in his book *On Safari* (1963). He had been received in audience by the Maharajah.

After a while I managed to explain that if it was possible I wanted to shoot scenes of animals in Nepal. At once the Maharajah's face lit up.

'You shoot?' he said.

I tried to explain that the sort of shooting we did was with cameras but he did not seem to understand the distinction I was making between this and big game hunting, and led me off to another room. It was really a hall, some forty feet long, and I realised it was the Maharajah's own trophy room. An artist had been brought all the way from Paris to cover one whole wall with an immense mural depicting, in heroic proportions, the Maharajah hunting rhinoceroses in the Himalayas. Along the length of the hall ran a series of low marble pillars. There must have been at least twenty on each side of the room. On each, expertly mounted, rested the stuffed head of a rhino.

That great room itself with its unspeakable mural was unpleasant enough, but those forty heads sent shudders down my spine. For they were the heads of East Indian rhinoceroses[1] and as far as I knew there were hardly forty still in existence.[2]

[1]There is no rhinoceros of this name, but he was obviously referring to the great Indian rhinoceros.

[2]This was a gross underestimate.

Suddenly this macabre collection seemed to expose the whole cult of big game hunting for the gruesome, useless business it is. As politely as I could I said to the Maharajah, 'You are aware, of course, Your Highness, that there are very, very few of these animals left and that when you have shot the last of them the whole species will then be extinct.'

He took his time to reply and then turned to me and winked. 'I think you will find', he said, 'that there will be just enough to last me my lifetime.'

Even so, the rhino was still common thirty years ago in many parts of Nepal and in the Sikkim *terai*. But with such organized slaughter, numbers began to deplete. A slow breeder, the ancient animal could never catch up with the losses. In the late 1940s, the rhino was not to be seen in Nepal except in the Chitawan jungles, east of the Gandak river. External pressure began to be brought on the Nepal Government to protect the rhino.

As the numbers decreased, the value of the rhino's horn, most coveted of all its anatomy, increased. The meat and hide could be sold, but it was the false horn, which in an adult animal weighs from two to five pounds, that was of prime interest to poachers. It is false horn, because it is nothing but hair matted together so solidly as to appear and feel horn-like. The first poachers came with muzzle-loaders heavy enough to dispose of the rhino, or caught it in pits. The horn has been highly prized in the East from early times. It was endowed with a host of magical properties. In powdered form it is still today considered in east and south-east Asian pharmaceutical trades a most potent aphrodisiac. Old accounts describe how the horns were sold in the Calcutta market—the most important rhino horn market in Asia—for 'half their weight in gold' and how eventually most of them found their way to China. It is known that in the first quarter of this century, single horns were sold for prices higher than £150. Lee Merriam Talbot reported in 1955, during an investigation of the status of the three Asian rhinoceroses, that he saw individual merchants in south-east Asia offer prices as high as $2,500 for one horn. In Sumatra, one Chinese merchant was offering a new American automobile in trade for a whole rhinoceros.

The horn had also other uses. A small fragment enclosed in a charm and worn round the neck or wrist made the wearer invulnerable to enemies. Extraordinary properties were also credited, to a lesser extent, to other parts of the body. Chewing the dry meat gave immunity against dysentery. Drinking the urine was a certain cure for all skin diseases. A sliver of bone inserted in an incision made on the arm injected the rhino's enormous strength into the man. Local hill tribes such as the Lhotas still bury a piece of rhino bone in their fields for a good harvest. Plaster made of the dung cured all kinds of swellings. Soup from boiling the umbilical stump was a certain cure for rheumatic and arthritic complaints. The Rengmas, another tribe, believe shields made from rhino hide impregnable in battle. This tribe has the further curious belief that the rhino sleeps on very steep ground, hooking its horn round a tree to save itself from slipping. It is easy to see that the poor beast, with such superlative qualities in its fleshy make-up, simply invited trouble.

Lest it be thought that rhinoceros superstitions are all of Eastern origin, many of these beliefs were once widely held in Europe. Rhinoceros-horn cups, for instance, were used by kings and popes to show up poison in their drinks by making the drink froth, or even cracking the cup. Rhino horn was also prized as an internal medicine, particularly for complaints of the stomach, well beyond the Middle Ages. Therefore, with the price they have carried on their heads, and indeed other parts of their anatomy, the wonder is not that rhinos are rare but that they exist at all.

Projects in India and human settlement in Nepal have, from another direction, attacked the rhino by destroying its habitat. In India, it survives only in a few localized sanctuaries, chief among which are Kaziranga in Assam and Jaldapara in West Bengal. In Nepal, total disaster threatened it, as a sudden land rush to its haunts in the late 1950s and early 1960s began to overwhelm it. However, R. S. M. Willan, Chief Conservator of Forests in Nepal, reported in 1965 that illegal settlers had largely been removed from both the King Mahendra National Park and the Chitawan Wild Life Sanctuary—both of recent genesis—on the orders of the present King of Nepal, and as a consequence rhino seemed to be recovering somewhat, with many calves seen about. Now, the survivors in the valleys of the three rivers, Narayani (or Gandak), Rapti, and Reu, appear to be receiving a better measure of protection.

The rhino is a miracle of survival in the ruthless evolutionary process, in the disappearance of old life forms and unfolding of the new, a real present-day monster, but a peculiarly likeable one to those who have some degree of acquaintance with it. Kaziranga is an area of monstrous swamps and therefore an appropriate habitat for monsters. Each time I have visited it, it seemed worse than before, with more areas squelchy and spongy even where they were not covered with water treacherously overlaid with water-hyacinth and smelling to high heaven. This impression may not, however, correspond to fact; it simply seemed to me so.

The sanctuary lies on the south bank of the great river Brahmaputra, and the swamps are intermingled with great expanses of high, coarse grass, which can top fifteen feet or more, and open forest, watercourses, and reed beds in the north. On its south, it is bounded by the Diphlu river, which is close to and parallel with the Assam Grand Trunk Road, the main arterial highway in the State, beyond which are the Mikir Hills, of significance to it, as the wild life of the sanctuary seeks refuge on the hills when the flood waters of the Brahmaputra pour over the swamps in the monsoon. The hills are clothed with the semi-evergreen and rain forests typical of Assam, and offer good cover for the animals, but their danger is great during the period of migration when they are killed in large numbers by the waiting poachers.

The sanctuary can be entered at more than one place, but is most easily accessible at Kohora by a jeep track which runs through open ground and paddy fields, which act as a buffer zone between the sanctuary and the grazing lands of domestic livestock. Riding on an elephant in the thick grass, the grass looms over on all sides, and its sharp edges can cut into the flesh like a knife. On my first visit to Kaziranga in 1958, I saw my first rhino, a big bull, almost immediately on entering the sanctuary and while still on foot, making the transfer from jeep to elephant. I quickly scrambled on to my mount, a young female, and attempted to get near the rhino which was in a small, muddy pool. Due to some bad manoeuvring by the

G

mahout and the greed of my mount, who on that trip never lost an opportunity of stopping and stuffing herself noisily with masses of green food, we were too slow, and the rhino beat a squelchy retreat from the mud-pool. He was an old beast, and I could see his flanks and rear were studded with masses of tubercles, which are characteristic of adult animals and become more and more prominent with advancing age.

A mother rhino and her calf on the far side of a *bheel*, as a small lake-swamp is called in these parts, made an interesting group. Rhino calves keep with their mothers for three years or more. The cow does not breed during this period, and a female therefore gives birth to a calf only every four or five years—a slow breeding rate. Cow rhinos with young calves are known to have unpredictable tempers, and remembering the story that had been told to me the previous evening of the American visitor to the sanctuary whose elephant had been determinedly pursued by a mother rhino till she had inflicted a severe cut in the elephant's side, I did not consider it prudent to press too close an acquaintance with this mother. From where I was, she appeared to be almost white, in contrast to the big fellow I had seen before who was the usual ashy-grey, but this was due to the tricks of the early morning light and the ground mist which still hung about. The great onehorned rhino inflicts injuries with its long lower teeth and not with its horn, as is generally believed. This is done by a quick side movement, and a terrible wound can result. I have seen the technique of it during later visits to Kaziranga, in not-too-serious tussles between bulls.

On this trip, as on others, a trying problem was to convey my wishes to the *mahout* for manoeuvring the elephant to positions advantageous for watching or photography. Once he has understood, and is willing, he has a far easier task translating these wishes to the elephant, who obeys without demur. More particularly in late years, *mahouts* have been slovenly, some not refraining from smoking *bidis*, or cigarettes made from rolling tobacco leaves, while conducting visitors into sanctuaries, or desisting from noisily clearing their throats and spitting, a nauseous habit. Casual visitors probably do not complain, but cannot be pleased, but how infuriating all this can be to one with more than casual interest or who has travelled a long way to film or photograph animals is difficult to put into words.

Wild life is not disturbed by an approaching elephant, but reacts to human noises or human-inspired smells. *Mahouts* may know all about their charges, the elephants, but often lack judgement in approaching wild animals, and worse, many of them just will not listen to suggestions as they consider themselves superior in junglecraft to any visitor.

Twice I was exceptionally close to rhinos in wallows, but these were by accident rather than by design. On both occasions, as my elephant cleared the tall grass, the wallow was at her feet, with the rhino in it. Both incidents ended with the rhinos steadily backing from the muddy water into the thick grass with ponderous, clumsy movements, their great weight causing their feet to slip and slither in the mud and the slush. They kept their piggy eyes on the elephant while accomplishing this retreat, puffing and snorting their disapproval of this invasion of their special hideout.

On another day, I entered the sanctuary from its south-western side, and the memory of the unspoilt wilderness of that area will always remain with me. Once we broke from tall grass into a clearing where the grass had recently been burnt, and in the centre of the clearing was a large rhino bull cropping the new shoots that had sprouted after the fire. He soon saw us and trotted off picking his feet off the ground daintily—it is possible to get this impression—stopping a couple of times to look back and see if he was being followed. Then there was another big bull who was unhurriedly cropping grass in an over-grown clearing. Terry and June Bassett, from Canada, mounted on another elephant, were anxious to film a rhino at close quarters. Their *mahout* urged his elephant as close to the rhino as he would permit. The rhino remained unprovoked, and had been finally driven to the edge of the grass jungle, where he stood his ground for a minute or two. He pawed the ground, looked formidable, and it seemed he might resent being pushed off his ground in this way. However, nothing happened and, wheeling round, he disappeared into the grass.

Often on the backs of rhinos were cattle egrets, pied mynas, or both, valets of the animal kingdom. Appropriately, it was Herodotus, the father of zoology, who first wrote of this associa-tion of a small creature with a big one. In his account of Egypt he wrote:

The crocodile is a foe to all birds and beasts, but the courser, which does it a service. For, living in the water, it gets its mouth full of leeches, and when it comes out and opens its mouth to the westerly breeze, the courser goes in and gobbles up the leeches, which good office so pleases the saurian that it does the courser no harm.

There are many such associations in the world of wild animals.

My last visit to Kaziranga was made in summer 1965 with Diana and our boys. The evening of our first entry into the sanctuary was hot and the distant rumble of thunder from behind the hills broke the silence in the still air. We soon arrived at the brink of a large expanse of swamp, almost completely covered with water-hyacinth. There before us was a pair of rhino, bull and cow, then beyond them a big bull, and yet another pair in an arm of the swamp on the far side. What a first reception to rhino-land it was to them! The filming which followed involved a great deal of elephant-manoeuvring, but the rhino were patient, and so it was accomplished with a good measure of success.

On a subsequent sortie on my own, I saw many rhino, and they were a cheering sight after the heavy loss to poachers in late 1964 and early 1965, when some twenty animals had been reported killed. Four rhino were brawling in a swamp, but hastily squelched their way out of it as I moved in on the elephant. In front of us materialized a great fellow who decided to go on with his morning ablutions despite the intrusion. Very deliberately, he sank into the water, which smelled very rank, till only his nostrils and ears were visible. We went right up to him, and beyond a show of faint interest in his piggy eyes, he was not disturbed in the least. Then there was another bull on the far shore of the same swamp who was equally nonchalant. He did not even deign to look at us as we drew near and stood by him. It is difficult to tell bull and cow rhinos apart, unless one is close enough. When at last I left the sanctuary, it was with the wish that the rhinos would ever thus remain placid and prehistoric in their last important refuge.

One local notable put the annual loss of rhino to poachers at thirty animals. In the 1964–65 scare, the carcasses were all found in the northern part of the sanctuary, and in one period of intensive search, thirteen carcasses and over fifty poachers' pits were said to have been discovered. In all, there were a hundred pits. Visitors to the sanctuary are shown around the southern fringe only, and the interior or the northern part which is waterlogged is seldom visited even by range staff owing to difficulties of terrain. Poachers accordingly cross the Brahmaputra from the north and gain ingress into the sanctuary. As an aftermath of the poaching, even as late as the time of our visit, May 1965, the bazaars on the borders of the sanctuary were rife with rumours of the money involved, said to be in the region of Rs. 4 *lakhs*. After the discovery of the carcasses and pits, the ensuring publicity was perhaps what brought the depredations to a temporary halt—temporary because the activities will no doubt be resumed should a favourable opportunity present itself. This nefarious work will cease only when the demand for rhino horn disappears, and as this is not likely to happen for a long time yet, the rhino is dependent entirely on the effectiveness of the protection given to it in the meantime. Unregistered animal dealers told me that year that a good-sized rhino horn was worth, in Calcutta, anything from Rs. 5,000 to Rs. 20,000, there apparently being grades of horn, appreciated only by connoisseurs of rhino products. They were unwilling to talk about the poaching bonanza, but vaguely indicated that the enterprise was financed by a Calcutta businessman. The ultimate destinations of the horns were said to be China, Hong Kong, and south-east Asia. With such big money involved, no wonder the poachers consider the risks worth taking.

The Government of Assam annually auctions horns recovered from rhino carcasses in the sanctuary and other reserves—these animals may have died from natural causes, or as a result of fights, or from predation. I have doubts about the ethics, or indeed the wisdom, of these auctions, despite the substantial income that is derived from it. After all, the Government sells something it knows to be utterly worthless. I wonder if the total destruction of the horns in public, announced and notified, would not have a long-range effect in demonstrating how useless they really are for any purpose.

Kaziranga, like the Hluhluwe Reserve in the Union of South Africa, had its rhino personalities. The most famous of them was 'Burra Goonda' (corruption of 'Burra Gaenda' or 'Big Rhino') who died in 1953. No one knew how old he was, but for the last fifteen years of his life he hardly left the locality he favoured on the southern fringe of the sanctuary, and visitors were assured of a close view of him either placidly wallowing in a mudpool or grazing peacefully amongst domestic animals on the verge of the sanctuary. He had many scars of battle with other rhinos, but at this period had become so gentle that with care he could be approached closely on foot. He was Kaziranga's most photographed rhino. The *mahouts* still tell a story, apocryphal no doubt, of how once a brave army officer actually hand-fed him with grass and then slapped him on his rump as much as to say, 'Well done, old boy.' The riding elephants of the time knew him, and he knew them.

After his death, his place was taken by another old bull, 'Kankatta', or 'Torn-ear'. From being an aggressive animal, he settled down to the vacated number one position and lived for four years.

The Jaldapara Sanctuary in north Bengal is, after Kaziranga, the rhino's most important refuge in India. The cover is thick, and the interior unexploited. Unfortunately, however, it is in a strategic area and, in the event of conflict between India and her northern or eastern neighbour, will be in the direct line of fire. With the Chinese invasion of 1962, huge army encampments sprung up everywhere in the region, some being set up within the sanctuary at Baradabri preceded by heavy tree-felling. As always when fighting men move in, poaching increased, and I saw many poachers' pits when I visited the sanctuary in October 1963. However, in 1965, the army was finally persuaded to leave after protracted negotiations, and when I was again in the sanctuary in October that year, things seemed to have much improved.

In 1963 I had taken my family with me, and after spending a couple of days at Chilapata and finding it too far away for daily visits to the sanctuary, we camped at Kodalbasti, a little-known Garo village just outside it. To enter the thick jungle of the sanctuary, the mountain torrent of the Torsa had to be crossed on elephant-back. Some arms of the river were shallow, but others were crashing floods after the plentiful monsoon rains of that year. Our riding elephants were in considerable difficulty, and the crossings became hazardous as the water came up to the pads on which we were seated and swirled and poured past carrying driftwood and boulders with it. The elephants, urged by the *mahouts*, knew what to do. They turned in the heaving waters, never more than just a little at a time, to face the flood and slowly sidled to safety on the other shore. This they did at each tumultuous crossing, but the experience was not pleasant, till finally we had to give it up as too dangerous and nerve-racking.

From the river bed, the snow-capped Himalayas were always visible and made a magnificent setting to a very lovely area. Silver-tipped grass on the islands in the river bed waved gently in the breeze, and the only sound was the crash and tumble of the water. The grass was exceedingly tall and the under-growth very lush after the rains. The jungle was impassable in places, and the elephants tore their way through, knocking down whole trees where it was necessary, never putting a foot wrong, so that their progress was a wondrous thing to watch. Not a glimmer of animal life showed anywhere, but one sensed the unrest of secret lives in the jungle. Lianas and creepers festooned and overhung our path, and the elephants neatly grasped them in their trunks and flung them aside, while, if some fell back to obstruct our passage, the *mahouts* used their sharp-bladed *kukris*, or daggers, to telling effect. These men carried on subdued and affectionate conversations with their charges, but for reasons beyond our comprehension suddenly stung them into obeying orders with blunt stabbing daggers. We have observed this repeatedly, and the slight wounds on the top of the head are never allowed to heal fully, and the *mahouts* seemed to be keeping them deliberately open to receive the stabbing blows to intimidate the elephants. I have spoken about this to forest officers and wild life wardens, and they have agreed it was an undesirable practice, but for some reason nothing is done about it. This was the one distressing part of elephant-back travel.

Where possible, we followed rhino paths, which were often tunnel mazes ploughed in the thick undergrowth by the ponderous beasts. And suddenly we saw our rhino. We were plunging through thick and very tall grass which topped the elephants' backs by a few feet, when my tusker, who was leading, came face to face with a big bull rhino. The surprise was mutual. There was a confused noise of snorts and I could not tell which snort came from which animal. The two giants of the animal world faced each other for a few seconds. The tusker was steady and held his ground, but the rhino's heart gave way and he wheeled right round into the black tunnel from which he had emerged. The elephant whiffed disdain and started to follow him, and the smaller female elephant with Diana and our younger son began to move up too. We had advanced a few steps when something rushed and moved in the tunnel. The rhino peered out and as suddenly turned again, and I had a last glimpse of his hindquarters as he disappeared. Soon, movement in the undergrowth told us that he had doubled back and was moving fast and away from us, perhaps to a favourite feeding ground of wild ginger and marsh reeds to restore his self-respect. Our then five-year-old, not a bit afraid, urged us after the beast. But circumstances were not propititious for a chase. I had hastily to ask the *mahouts*, as they prepared to carry out the imperious order of that small voice, not to attempt a follow-up into that tunnel of vegetation, black as Hades, and just then the rhino's room seemed preferable to his company.

Another trip I made into the sanctuary with the older boy stands out in my memory for the way in which our riding elephant, a big female and a lovable one, 'Kamaladevi'—each morning she used to come to us for titbits, shrill squeals announcing her arrival—herself tried to locate a rhino for us. It was perfectly amazing how she responded to her *mahout*'s whispered commands. He often held consultations with her as to what we should do next, and the decision, it seemed, did not always lie with him. Once we were hot on the trail of a rhino, and my son and I followed with astonishment the way she picked up his scent trail, now selecting this side of a forked path, and now the other, now examining a thick undergrowth by lifting the masses of bush and leaves and creepers, and now whooshing before a tangle of vegetation, daring the rhino to come out. It was a quarter of an hour of wonderful flurry, and though we did not find the rhino, it became a memorable experience.

In Nepal, much of the main rhino area has been affected by human invasion, as mentioned before, though a recovery has been reported. Multi-purpose development projects are planned, and how effectively the rhino and other wild life will be safeguarded in the changing years of the future remains to be seen.

The estimated world population of the great onehorned rhino is now thought to be about 745, connecting the figures of Gee (1963), Willan (1965 for Nepal), and J. J. Spillet (1967). Of this number, Assam has 525, Bengal 55, and Nepal 165. Again, of Assam's number, Kaziranga alone is thought to have 400. The other Assam sanctuaries with rhino are Manas, Sonairupa, Laokhowa, Orang, and one or two more very small reserves. A very few rhinos also live outside these sanctuaries, but their continued survival is uncertain with the poachers continually after them.

Kaziranga is, therefore, the rhino's most important survival home by far. It is also the best looked after of the Assam sanctuaries. Even more needs to be done to ensure its permanence. Poachers apart, the pressure of human population on its borders is a threat which could lead to excision of small parts from it from time to time, if not guarded against. Demands have many times been made for more grazing area for the proliferating domestic livestock, and this problem, I was told, had frequently figured in the manifestos issued by local political parties during elections. Danger also exists from the proximity of cattle, in that any disease carried into the sanctuary by them will have serious consequences. Surveillance itself, within the sanctuary, has also to be improved by provision of facilities for the ranger staff to patrol the area which is both large and difficult—such as wheeled transport, and boats for use in the northern riverside parts. The annual flooding is also a grave problem, as it leads to loss of wild life during its migration to higher ground. But it may be a mixed blessing, for the floods may be of benefit in maintaining the sort of habitat favoured by both rhino and buffalo, which latter is the sanctuary's second most sought-after wild animal.

The great Indian rhino is of extraordinary interest to natural history. It is incapable of adapting itself to new circumstances or environment. In the final event, whether it will survive all the assaults on its continued existence will depend on the effective adoption of a policy which will safeguard it from every angle. There is no room for complacency with a world population of

only 745—and remembering that the other two Asiatic rhinoceroses, the lesser onehorned or Javan and the twohorned or
Sumatran, also lived in India but do so no longer. The first of
these disappeared from Indian limits probably around the turn
of the century, but the latter is believed to have survived as late
as the mid-1930s in the Mizo Hills.

The great rhino is a truly harmless animal, and does no
damage whatever to human interests in the places where it still
lives. It is often misrepresented as being aggressive or attacking
on sight. Its blind, withering charge is delivered only when it
believes it is in danger or when it is surprised in its haunts.
Of course it is then very dangerous. Otherwise it is neither
truculent, nor a crop-raider. It is one of India's most spectacular
animals, a left-over from bygone ages, and a source of mystery
and wonder to all who see it in its natural home.

V
EXTINCT AND NEAR-EXTINCT

> . . . one of the greatest crimes of which man is capable is to permit the extermination of any form of wildlife. A species is a unique organism, one that has been produced by the action of natural forces through the ages and one that, when lost, is irreplaceable.
>
> IRA N. GABRIELSSON

FOR MANY YEARS I had searched records, reports, and sporting accounts for mention of the Indian cheetah (*Acinonyx jubatus*) in the wild state. I had examined every report on wild life of the Forest Departments of the various States to which I was given access, and even followed up newspaper stories of the shooting of a cheetah. Finally, in 1959, I arrived at the only possible conclusion—that the cheetah was extinct in the wild, and I reported it in an article which appeared in *The Field*.

The last reliable mention of a live wild cheetah was made by K. M. Kirkpatrick who reported seeing one on the road near Chandragiri, in a low hilly tract in the heart of southern India, on the night of 28–29 March 1952, while he was out driving. There have been occasional newspaper stories since of the shooting of a cheetah, but these, followed up, always led to a leopard, and only showed that most people and many sportsmen in India do not know the difference between the two animals.

The only other evidence of the existence of the cheetah in the wild after 1950, came to me as I was composing parts of this book in winter 1965, when I was presented with a copy of the book *Wilberforce Our Monkey* (1958) by its author, James Milne, when we, both grass-widowers, were living in the Calcutta Club. I came across a passage describing an encounter with a cheetah on the Orissa-Hyderabad (now Andhra Pradesh)

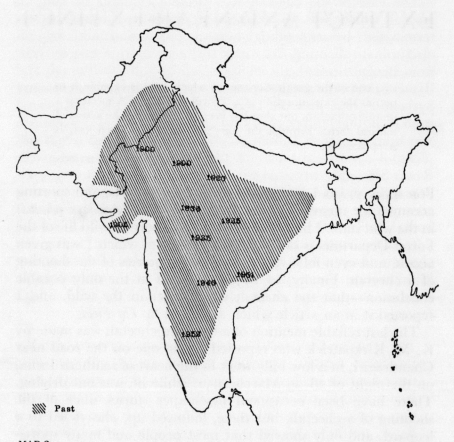

MAP 2

Past distribution of the Indian cheetah, with probable dates of extinction in the various tracts. The cheetah is now extinct in India

border in 1951, a personal experience of Milne himself. I discussed it with him soon after I had read it, and he had no doubt that he had seen a cheetah, though he could not vouch for the villagers' reports about there being more cheetahs in the area.

The case of the cheetah is a striking example of how an animal which was so extensively distributed could be exterminated by expanding human population and by indiscriminate shooting. Its range was countrywide east to west, from Bengal through the plains of upper India to Punjab and Baluchistan in the north, whence it extended through Persia and Syria to Africa, and the Deccan in the south. It disappeared from Rajasthan and central India about the turn of the century, and from the upper Indian plains around 1920. But it was still plentiful towards the end of the last century in some parts. R. A. Sterndale wrote in his great work *Natural History of the Mammalia of India and Ceylon* (1884), 'places in which it is most common are Jeypur in Upper India and Hyderabad in Southern India'.

It is believed that, after the plains of upper India, the cheetah disappeared from Bundelkhand and the Mahadeo Hills around 1935, and from upper Deccan around 1940. Dunbar Brander wrote in his *Wild Animals in Central India* (1931),

The Hunting Leopard[1] has now almost disappeared from the Province[2] without apparent reason, and I only know of three animals having been procured in the last twenty years. In territories outside the Province, especially in the north, they are commoner. Rumours of their existence in parts of Berar, the Seoni Plateau, and Saugar, still persist, and it is possible that one or two may still persist.

Writing of a hunt in 1932 in the Princely State of Talcher, in Orissa, in his book *Kingdoms of Yesterday*, Sir Arthur Cunningham Lothian said, 'In Talcher one day, when out for tiger, I fired at an animal moving through the jungle, and found to my great

[1] Another name by which the cheetah was known.

[2] Central Provinces, the present Madhya Pradesh in essence.

regret that I had shot a specimen of that very rare animal the Indian cheetah'.

The position after the 1920s was that if there were wild survivors in some numbers, the middle and lower Deccan seemed the last likely homes. They probably existed in the flat country where the Tungabhadra dam came to be built. But with the construction of that dam in the late 1940s and early 1950s, all wild life in the tract disappeared, even the abundant blackbuck, and also the wolf and the chinkara.

It is a significant fact that although much was being said and promised in the early 1950s about conservation of wild life in the country, no measures at all were taken even to save a very few of the cheetah, if not at that time possible for living in a natural state, at least for a breeding nucleus under controlled conditions, from which it might well have been possible to liberate a small number into a plains reserve at a future date. Instead, the cheetah was talked about. At the first meeting of the Indian Board for Wild Life in November 1952, the then Union Minister of Agriculture called for assigning special priority for the protection of the cheetah in central India, from which it had already gone. Again, at the Board's meeting of 1955, speakers were still talking of 'bold experimentation' to preserve the cheetah, after it had become extinct.

The cheetah's habitat of open bushland and boulder and low hill country paved the way for its extinction. This kind of country attracted both human expansion by extended cultivation and the shoot-on-sight type of sportsman. Once the numbers were reduced beyond the biological minimum necessary in nature for existence, its extinction was only a matter of time. The last few did not have to be shot. The cheetah also, very likely, was a slow breeder—not much is known of its breeding habits.

It certainly existed in big numbers. The naturalist Jardine has stated that cheetahs were kept in thousands by the Moghul Emperors for sporting purposes. One wonders, with so many captive cheetahs, what the cheetah population of India must have been then. The animals were kept by most Indian Princes and noblemen and were a necessary adjunct to noble status. The Kolhapur[1] ménage of hunting cheetahs was famous in the

[1] A Princely State between Goa and Poona.

Princely days before the last war. The animal was so much in demand that there had even grown up a professional class of cheetah-catchers whose only business was the catching of it and its training for hunting down antelope and small game. It is interesting to read that these men caught only the adult animals and considered cubs difficult to train for purposes of the chase. The catching of cheetah involved a special technique, and I will quote one amusing account from *The Asian* of 22 July 1880, written by 'Deccanee Bear'.

Arrived at the spot the bullocks were soon relieved of their burden, and the work commenced. The nooses were of the same kind as those used for snaring antelope, made from the dried sinews of the antelope. These were pegged down in all directions, and at all angles, to a distance of twenty-five to thirty feet from the tree. The carts and bullocks were sent off into a road about half a mile away. An ambush was made of bushes and branches some fifty or sixty yards away, and here, when the time came, I and three Vardis ensconced ourselves. I have sat near some dirty fellows in my life, but the stench of those three men baffles description; you could cut it with a knife. I could not smoke, so had to put up with the several smells until I was nearly sick. At last the sun commenced to sink, and the men who were looking round in all directions, suddenly pointed in the direction of the north. Sure enough there were four cheetahs skying away and playing together about 400 yards off; they came closer and closer, when they stopped about 100 yards off, looking about as if they suspected danger. However, they became reassured, and all raced away as hard as they could in the direction of the tree. Two were large and the other two smaller; the larger had the best of the race, and were entangled by all four feet before they knew where they were. The Vardis made a rush. I did the same, but in a second was flat on the ground, having caught my feet in the nooses. One of the men came and released me from my undignified position, and I could then see how the cheetahs were secured. A country blanket was thrown over the head of the animal, and the two fore and hind legs tied together. The carts had come up by this time; a leather hood was substituted for the blanket—a rather ticklish operation, during which one man was badly bitten in the hand. The cheetahs know how to use their teeth and claws. Having been securely fastened on the carts, and the nooses collected, we started for camp, which we reached about eight in the evening. I was much pleased with what I had seen and learnt, but it took me a long time to get the smell of the Vardis out of my head. The next morning I went to see the cheetahs and found that they had been tied spread-eagle fashion on the carts, and with their hoods firmly tied. They were a pair, and in all probability the parents of the two smaller ones. Women and children are told off to sit all day long close to the animals, and keep up a conversation, so that they should get accustomed to the human voice. The female was snarling a good deal, the male being much quieter; they go through various gradations of education, and I was told that they would be ready to be unhooded and worked in about six months' time.

The mode of hunting with a cheetah was as follows. It was taken to bush or open country in which antelopes lived, hooded and chained in an open bullock-drawn cart, or in later days in a four-wheeled wagon without sides. When the antelope were within about 200 yards, the cheetah was released. It immediately marked down one of the grazing animals for its quarry, and invariably ran it down in a short distance. If it failed to do so, it simply gave up. When an antelope was killed, the cheetah was rewarded by its keeper with a bowl of blood drawn from the slit throat of the victim. It quickly lapped this up, when it was hooded again and returned to the cart or wagon.

I give an eye-witness account of hunting with cheetah, which, as things turned out, must have been one of the last of its kind, with the disappearance of the Princely States soon after. Suydam Cutting writes in his book *The Fire Ox and Other Years* (1947) of cheetah-hunting in Kolhapur. There were thirty-five cheetahs in the cheetah house—African cheetahs as Indian cheetahs were already unobtainable.

A cheetah, still hooded,[1] was lying on a platform built into the car at about the level of my knees. His keeper, crouched

[1]Hunting cheetahs wore hoods always except when fed, exercised, or put to hunt.

on the running-board, a precarious perch, had to keep his eyes on the animal and also get out at times and have a look at the trappy ground. On we careered, sometimes on lanes, but more often across open country where our thirty-five miles an hour was a dizzy speed. Everyone held on like mad.

Having found a herd[1], we manoevured for a proper position. Then began the real strategy. In confronting a large herd, an attempt was always made to detach the males— quarries for the cheetahs. They were kept in a continuous stampede. Since they did not run in a straight line, the car bucketing along was able to keep up with them. . . .

Then, with everything perfectly timed by the Maharajah, the car stopped. The cheetah was unloaded, and hustled out on the grass. For half a minute he stood there sizing up the situation. At a gentle, slow lope he started off towards the herd. The blackbuck, about two hundred yards away, began to move off. The field was alive with galloping forms, their bounds increasing progressively in length. By now the cheetah had chosen his particular quarry. He rushed to-wards it at incredible speed.

The quarry, realizing too late that he could not match the cheetah's speed, attempted a downhill slope. The cheetahs prefer to run uphill: going down they are liable to a false aim and then a bad tumble.

Undaunted by this manoeuver, the cheetah soon overtook his buck. He sprang with front paws directed at the hind-quarters of the quarry. The violence of this blow threw the animal. Then the cheetah caught him by the throat.

At this point we arrived on the scene. The cheetah lay full-length, with the buck's throat held tightly in its slightly curved canines. Gradually the victim ceased his violent attempts to tear himself loose. He was choked to death. The cheetah lay perfectly still in apparent ecstasy. Slowly he opened and closed his great greenish eyes, gently emitting a soft, rumbling purr.

The cheetah was allowed to feast on one hindquarter of the buck. Then he was gently and firmly led aside while one of the attendants disembowelled the victim. Some of the blood and

[1]Of blackbuck.

H

the steaming viscera, placed in a long spoonlike bowl, was offered to the cheetah. This was his reward, and he seemed quite satisfied.

There was never any organized hunting of the cheetah in India, as in the case of the tiger, the rhino or the buffalo, and this perhaps was the only reason why it survived for as long as it did. It is a highly specialized animal for running down fast-fleeing quarry, and it is without doubt the fastest thing on four legs for the first couple of furlongs. Francois Boulière in his book *The Natural History of Mammals* (1955) gives an instance of a cheetah covering 700 yards in 20 seconds—an astonishing speed of more than 71 miles an hour! In full gallop, the animal has been timed to attain 45 miles an hour immediately upon starting! Such an animal would have been at a serious disadvantage anywhere where it would not have been able to use its magnificent speed. Therefore, it would seem that there was no attempt made by the last survivors to retreat, in the face of persecution, to thick cover, where additionally the natural prey of the cheetah, antelope and other small beasts, would be absent.

Some years ago, there was a proposal to import the African cheetah and settle it in open, dry tracts in central, west, and south India, preferably where blackbuck was available. The experiment was fortunately never made, for it would have been doomed to failure. In such tracts, the cheetah would be killed off as soon as it was put there, as no effective protection can be given at the present time. Moreover, blackbuck has also generally gone from such areas, and has shown distinct signs of seeking thicker cover. The chapter of the Indian cheetah, therefore, must be taken as closed. There are perhaps a very small number still alive in captivity, but no attempt has been made to find out if the species can be saved, at least under captive conditions, by getting such animals together.

Is there a difference between the African and Indian cheetahs? Perhaps not. I have not seen enough of either to form an opinion. It may be that, as in the case of the lions from the two areas, the largest African cheetah was bigger than the biggest Indian one. In Africa, too, cheetahs are very much on the decline, the vast extents of the national parks and game reserves alone having prevented their extinction thus far. African parks and reserves include great stretches of open and bush country, while in India, the sanctuaries are not only of small spread, but also do not include the kind of habitat favoured by the cheetah.

The lion was once widely distributed in Asia, from Asia Minor and Arabia through Persia to India. It is now reduced to a tiny remnant in the Gir Forest in the Gujerat peninsula, leaving out the few in the Chandraprabha Sanctuary in Uttar Pradesh. In the Indian sub-continent it had a wide range over northern India, as far east as Bihar, with the Narmada river marking the southern limit. T. C. Jerdon said in his *The Mammals of India* (1874) that he had heard of lions being killed south of that river many years previously, but the animals were probably stray ones which had temporarily crossed the river.

Even before the close of the last century, the Indian lion (*Panthera leo persica*) had gone from all of its range except Gir. The probable years of its extermination regionwise appear to be, Bihar 1814, Cutch 1830, Delhi 1834, Bahawalpur 1842, Eastern Vindhyas and Bundelkhand 1865, central India and Rajasthan 1870, and Western Aravallis 1880.

From 1880 to the turn of the century, there were supposed to be less than a dozen animals left in Gir. There is one theory that the then Nawab of Junagadh, in whose territory the Gir Forest was, and who was strictly protecting them, gave a low number in order that pressure might not be brought on him by his fellow Princes or the Viceroy or the Governors of British India for a lion shoot. Whatever it may have been, the lion was saved and, as its shooting came to be accepted as improvident, slowly recovered. In 1950, a census put the population at 240, in 1955 at 290, in 1963 at 280, and in 1968 at 162 (P. Joslin and K. Hodd). The latest figure does not imply a drastic reduction since 1963, but more likely indicates the application of improved counting methods and that the earlier census was an overestimate.

As discussed in the chapter on tigers, the tiger had nothing to do with the disappearance of the lion from northern and central India. The reason was that the lion lived in comparatively open country, where it was easily hunted. It lacked the cunning of the tiger, failed to take the evasive action necessary for survival, was partly diurnal in habit and, above

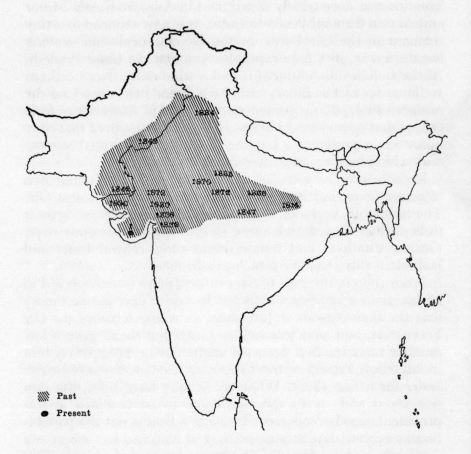

MAP 3
Past and present distribution of the Indian lion, with the probable dates of
extermination in the different regions. It survives only in the Gir Sanctuary,
marked '1'

all, was the most coveted trophy of the hunters, who were in the main Indian Princes and noblemen or British officers.

In 1952, the Indian Board for Wild Life recommended that a second home should be found for the lions, so that in case of a major natural or other disaster in Gir the species will not be wiped out. There was difficulty in finding this home, which had to be ecologically suitable and within the former range of the lion. Finally, the Chandraprabha Forest in southern Uttar Pradesh was settled upon.

The area of this forest, made into a sanctuary, is only thirty square miles, and it is therefore incapable of supporting a large lion population. Still, I suppose it was a question of this or nothing. Accordingly, a Gir lion and two lionesses were released there in December 1957. The three animals soon settled down, and cubs were born to one or the other of the females in succeeding years. When I was in Chandraprabha in 1964, there were eleven lions living. A few had been shot by poachers or had died from unknown causes within or outside the sanctuary. The sanctuary is fenced for the most part, but the lions occasionally stray out into the surrounding open forest country. Fortunately, at no time had the lions any brush with human beings. A permanent fear was that if any humans were killed, political capital would be made out of it.

The sanctuary seemed thinly populated by herbivores, probably as a result of the disturbance caused by the teak plantations which had been introduced within it. I wondered at the thoughtlessness of it; the area had been picked for the lions, was already not large, and yet the plantations were pushed into it, causing an immediate loss of equilibrium. Further inroads had been checked, I was told.

The Gir Forest Reserve was upgraded to a Wild Life Sanctuary in 1967. Its problems, however, remain. These have been the slow diminution of the forest, in spite of the restrictions against tree-felling and cutting, the possibility of disease in a confined area, and poaching, if not within the sanctuary, outside it by means of enticements through tie-ups of cattle. Wild prey is scarce, and as a result lions help themselves to domestic livestock, of which there is more in the area than economically desirable, but which nevertheless represents a source of wealth to its owners. There are villages within the sanctuary, and from time to time there have been reports of lions being poisoned by the villagers who resent losing their cattle to the lions. The great number of livestock which graze in reach of the lions is of course an open invitation to the latter to obtain easy meals.

It is to be hoped that, with the constitution of the Gir as a sanctuary, more modern management methods will be applied. It is mostly thorn forest, with little exploitable timber, and this should be in its favour. It would seem essential that poaching of sambar, chital, nilgai, and pig is eradicated as far as possible, so that there are more of them to provide food for the lions. Livestock grazing should also be reduced to save habitat, and to give less cause for grievance from the villagers and graziers.

The clouded leopard (*Neofilis nebulosa*) is one of the most beautiful of the cats. I have not seen it in the wild state, but have studied specimens in the Alipore Zoo in Calcutta where, despite all the care which its remarkable Superintendent, R. K. Lahiri, lavishes on his charges, they have not had long spans of life. The management of this zoo, incidentally, is in a class of its own in India—in the face of heavy odds—and the life histories and feeding habits of individual animals which Lahiri maintains teach a lesson of their own.

The clouded leopard is today one of the world's rarest, and most elusive, beasts. At the best of times it was thinly distributed, and occurred mainly in the Malay peninsula, extending westward into the dense evergreen forests of Burma, Yunnan, Assam, Sikkim, and Nepal. With the destruction of large forest tracts in Assam or their opening up, it seems to have fallen increasingly to poachers, and unusual quantities of its pelt appeared in Calcutta in the 1950s. The fur is soft and very beautiful, expensive, and much sought-after, and can still be seen in the shops of the leading furriers. A made-up lady's coat may fetch Rs. 10,000 or more. Its export is prohibited, but it is sent off nevertheless under other names, and the customs are no experts and often cannot be bothered.

Its secretive habits, and nocturnal and largely arboreal life, combined with its rarity, have made it a creature of mystery. Very little indeed is known about it, and apart from those in the Alipore Zoo, few specimens have reached zoological gardens.

Reference in sporting literature is scant, and I have come across five instances only: G. H. Peacock in his book *A Game-Book for Burma and Adjoining Territories*, A. W. Strachan in his *Mauled by a Tiger* (1933), H. B. Gabb in the *Journal of the Bengal Natural History* in 1945, Col. H. S. Wood in the same *Journal* in 1948, and Hari Dang in *Cheetal* in 1967.

Its markings resemble those of the marbled cat (*Felis marmorata*), another member of the cat family which is as elusive as the clouded leopard and with which the latter has sometimes been confused. The ground colour is light yellowish-grey, and on it are darkish blotches which may be regarded as extensions in size of the rosettes of the leopard, giving a clouded, marbled pattern to the skin. These blotches are nowhere as many in number as the leopard's rosettes. They are of the largest size at the shoulders and on the sides, decreasing gradually in dimensions towards the hindquarters and coalescing as spots on the top of the head and on the legs. Other features are the longish spots on the middle of the back, the two dark stripes on the cheeks, and the black, broken rings on the tail. The canines are large for the animal's size, and are most representative among the cats of today of the great development in their ancestor, the formidable sabretoothed tiger. The forelegs are short and thickset, which gives it a somewhat squat look. The tail is what attracts most on first appearance, for it is very long, very fat, and carries plenty of fur.

A curious thing is the extreme hardness of the pads. Other cats have soft pads which enable them to stalk their prey in silence. The clouded leopard has no need for soft pads as it catches its prey by dropping down on them from trees. I have heard it being called, no doubt on account of this, '*bandar bagh*', which means 'monkey tiger', by tribesmen.

It presumably lives on small animals, and perhaps a bird or two it is able to catch in its arboreal home.

It represents the kind of animal for which no direct protection can be given. Its survival can be strengthened only by leaving parts of its habitat of evergreen forest free from exploitation, and by keeping a watch on the furs offered for sale.

Another member of the cat family—I call it a cat by virtue of its latest classification—whose survival is problematic is the elusive caracal. Its placement through Indian natural history seems to have somewhat baffled zoologists. It went through *Felis caracal*, *Lynx caracal*, then *Caracal caracal* (Müller, first edition of S. H. Prater's *The Book of Indian Animals* (1948) when it was said to have been placed beyond dispute, to return once again to *Felis caracal* (Schreber, second edition of Prater's book, 1965). There is a hint of desperation in all this! It has been called a near-cat, a lynx almost, the Persian lynx, the red lynx, other lynxes besides, and is back as a good cousin cat. It is a supple and sinuous animal, and its outstanding features are the lynx-like ears, with the brush of fine hair on their tips, coloured jet black on the outside and white on the inside.

My acquaintance with this beast also is limited to captive animals. I had believed it to be an inhabitant of semi-arid areas till, after writing about it in *The Statesman* of Calcutta, R. L. Holdsworth said in a letter to that newspaper that he had shot three himself and seen another shot in the Siwalik Hills. Once widely ranging over much of western Asia and Africa, it is now thought that the caracal has disappeared from most of its former territory in India—Baluchistan, Sind, and Cutch, extending to Punjab, Rajasthan, and central India. It may be, as Holdsworth suggested in his letter, 'that the caracal has, with increased cultivation of the semi-desert, almost died out there but survives in the denser jungles of the U.P. and has adapted its life accordingly.' Subsequently, another letter from J. R. Upshon suggested that it may have infiltrated further east to the Orissa jungles, where he shot one.

A careless look might confuse the caracal with the common jungle cat (*Felis chaus*), and it is probable that many caracal have been shot as jungle cats. But distinguishing it from the true cats, the caracal, like the lynx, slopes down from back to front. The lack of the ruff of hair round the face and the longer tail further distinguish it from the lynx. There are special facial markings too. There are single elongated black spots above the eyes and towards the centre of the forehead, a less distinct stripe between these spots running through the width of the forehead, and black patches on the upper tips at the ends of the mouth. The body colour is that of slightly reddish sand such as one sometimes unexpectedly sees on river beds, with light spots on the white-furred belly. In the very young, and even more in

27 Fully trained cheetah being taken in a bullock cart for the hunt
28 The end of a hunt. The cheetah has brought down a blackbuck

29 Author's eldest son, Vishnu, with lion cubs born in Alipore Zoological Gardens, Calcutta.

30 Male blackbuck in Guindy Park

31 Chousingha female surprised in the act of being photographed in typical
   hill-grass country

32 Group of nilgai in thorn jungle

33 Common langur, black-faced, long-tailed monkey which lives all over India

34 Bonnet macaque, the little pale-faced monkey of strolling monkey-men.
Mother grooming young

35 Performing bonnet monkeys and strolling monkey man, Maithon, Bihar

36 Performing sloth bear, with
its owner, Maithon, Bihar

37 A termite hill, favourite
feeding ground of sloth
bear and pangolin

38 Giant Indian squirrel, Mudumalai Sanctuary

new-born kittens, the entire coat is said to be spotted, but I have not seen babies.

It is a remarkable fact that so little should have been recorded about the caracal, considering that it was tamed and employed to hunt small antelope and deer, hare, fox, and birds. Nothing seems to be known, for example, of its breeding habits. It has been said that the Princes used to keep numbers of the animal for hunting small game, somewhat like the cheetah, and also for matching one against another in a strange sport—pigeon-slaying. The two animals used to be let loose simultaneously into a flock of pigeons, and the one which killed the largest number before the birds were able to rise in the air was the winner—as good a bloodsport as any. On such occasions, its agility was said to be quite extraordinary. Its hunting speed too, while it fell short of the cheetah, was still phenomenal. The structure of the hind legs and feet is obviously responsible. Watching it in captivity, I could well believe it to be a creature of swiftness and stealth. Its easy, careless walk, the adroit way in which it climbed tree trunks and came down again, and the concentration with which it bolted down lumps of freshly killed meat snarling in obvious enjoyment, all showed its capabilities as a predator on small and medium-sized animals.

As an animal of such agility and swiftness, it would have little use for heavy, thick jungles, and the caracal normally lived in dry, open bush country interspersed with rock and grass. Here it could employ its speed and skill to catch its prey, its bird-capturing ability not limited to the ground, but including being able to spring several feet in the air and knock low-flying birds down. It may have retreated to thicker cover with loss of its open habitat, and no one knows what chances this cat-lynx has of survival in the changing forest scene of India. Not large and therefore not in the forefront of animals recommended for protection, it may well go the way of the cheetah. If that happens, an attractive, lively, and interesting animal will have been lost.

I should like to sound a note of warning on the decline of the blackbuck (*Antilope cervicapra*) which, though not in danger of extinction, is one of the animals which has been disappearing fastest, and cannot sustain such a loss rate much longer. It is being shot off the plains, and its numbers in the sanctuaries are very small; and even there, it is persistently pursued by the poacher. Its habitat is the scrub and the open plains, where it has fallen in thousands to every description of shooting, and very many tracts where it was common have been completely emptied of it.

It once lived in great herds, and there are nineteenth-century accounts of congregations of 8,000 to 10,000. The animals were still so numerous that Forsyth was able to write eighty years ago:

> Although many of them are shot by the village *shikaris* at night, and more speared and netted by the professional hunters called Pardis (who use a trained bullock in stalking round the herds to screen their movements), the resources of the natives are altogether insufficient, in a country favourable to them, to keep down the numbers of these prolific and wary creatures.

Blackbuck began to be shot in large numbers near military cantonments by British soldiers in the nineteenth and early twentieth centuries. Shooting them did not require much skill unless they had started to run. British army officers tried also to ride them down for spearing—an extension of the sport of pig-sticking—and though there are claims that this was done, it is unlikely that it was achieved except when the buck was at a disadvantage. No horse can match blackbuck on any kind of ground. Greyhounds were also tried and never caught the buck on anything like equal terms, but apparently this provided sport for the officers. There are also accounts of shooting blackbuck from camel-back, when the buck seem to have taken no notice of the hunter on the camel's back. Yet another method was employed by hill and jungle tribes. This was to chase the blackbuck into marshy ground, which they do not favour, and then despatch them with spears when they got bogged down and were unable to move. Snaring and netting, used for all herbivores, were also employed by the tribes.

Since the extinction of the cheetah, blackbuck are the fastest-moving of all wild life in India. To watch them in motion, the effortless beauty of it, is a thing to remember. They start off, when alarmed, in a series of light leaps and bounds, taking occasionally an imaginary giant gate in their stride, before settling to a magnificent gallop. They have been timed to run at sixty miles an hour when running flat out and, unlike the cheetah which is soon spent, can keep up this tremendous pace for mile after mile. Herds indeed have been followed, in the old days, for ten miles without their letting up. It is a curious fact of nature that despite the absolute overlordship of the male over his harem, the female can outrun and outlast the male in a straight-out contest. But woe unto the female who thus runs away from her lord! The buck can be rough when he wants with his wives. Their vitality is equally amazing, and wounded blackbuck have run with seemingly inexhaustible energy, to the despair and chagrin of the hunter who has missed his aim.

The elegance of a herd standing out in a plain is very striking. It is equalled by no other animal, not even by the chital, generally considered the most beautiful of all deer. Forsyth wrote, 'Suffice it to say, that not even in Africa—the land of antelopes—is there any species which surpasses the "black buck" in loveliness and grace.' The splendid spiralled horns topping the striking coloration of the body, dark brown turning to velvety black, abruptly changing to pure white in the underparts and chest, make the males the true sultans they are. The white patches round the eyes are also a characteristic feature of the adult animal.

I have watched males in rut in the months of February and March, when they collect as many females as possible in their harem, and fight savagely for their possession. The male at this time is an arrogant, pugnacious, and combative beast. He guards the ladies very zealously, drives away importunate smaller males, and is ever ready to take offence and fight any adult male who strays into his kingdom. He has, too, a characteristic strut, develops a mincing sort of gait, and throws his head backwards so that the splendid spiralled horns lie flat along the back. Repeatedly I have tried to approach a herd with the herd male in this condition, and he has met me with short, challenging grunts and tossing nostrils, and a male blackbuck with his face glands wide open is no mean antagonist.

Blackbuck exhibit an inquisitiveness which has been noted by many sportsmen. In late years, however, with increasing persecution, they have become more wary and ready to run.

Their hearing is only moderate, but they quickly detect movement with their eyes, when they show alarm by lifting up their
heads to watch. I knew a herd of blackbuck some years ago in
the Kanha National Park with which I grew to be on friendly,
but never familiar, terms. They would let me approach so near,
but no nearer. They grazed, generally, on a grass meadow across
a deep watercourse in front of the forest resthouse, up to about
eleven o'clock in the morning. Then they slowly retreated to the
shade of the *sal* trees of which the forest was mainly composed.
They would lie down for the day, rising again in the evening
about four o'clock. The master buck was a splendid beast. He
did not always keep with the herd, but whether he was around
or not, the herd was clearly his prize. In Kanha, blackbuck
have been poached badly, and have now been reduced to a
mere twenty head! Yet at one time they lived in herds of
thousands in this tract.

There is a herd of white blackbuck in the Madras Zoo, presented to it many years ago by the late Maharajah of Bhavnagar,
who specialized in the breeding of white strains of animals and
birds. Melanism, or complete black coloration, is also known in
blackbuck. In 1960, I wrote to the Madras Zoo for information
on the white herd, and received this written reply:

These beautiful little bucks and does are the most outstanding
gifts of H. E. the Maharajah of Bhavnagar, Governor of Madras.
After coming over to this Zoo, they have bred and fawned
here. The ancestors of this species are the fallow deer of
England with large horns. In all other respects they resemble
the spotted deer. It is difficult to acclimatize pure English
fallow deer in temperate climates but a series of such successive hybridizations produce a type of white deer, which thrive
well in temperate climates. Their hair is generally short and
smooth, the eyes bright and beaming with keenest power of
vision. They also possess a delicate sense of smell. They are
just like other deer. (!!)

Well! Blackbuck descended from fallow deer! And all the rest of
it! When I protested that fallow deer could not have produced
blackbuck, whatever the jugglery of 'hybridization', I received
a further letter which peremptorily ended the correspondence:

The information I gave was copied out from the Madras Zoo guide printed in 1951. However these white bucks were presented by the Maharajah of Bhavnagar originally. Hence it is suggested that the Maharajah may be contacted as he is the person who possessed the original stock.

I then wrote to the Maharajah, and received an informative reply from his 'A.D.C. in Charge of Birds and Animals', which duly confirmed that the white blackbuck did not descend from English fallow deer, but were the progeny of white animals which the Maharajah had collected over the years.

Since the disappearance of the cheetah, there are now no other predators of large size which live on the plains—the wolf too having more or less vanished. Man is now the blackbuck's only enemy. The blackbuck also, unfortunately, is too fond of feeding on growing crops of all kinds, though in its present numbers it in no way poses a threat to the cultivator's economy. But by coming close to cultivated fields, it is further killed by villagers.

Blackbuck require plenty of living space, a condition that is not likely to be had in the future. A herd of ten animals is a sizeable one today. The Wild Life Preservation Society of India in a project report in 1964 estimated that about 80,000 blackbuck lived in India in 1947, and this had fallen to about 8,000. This will serve to illustrate my statement that it is one of the fastest-disappearing Indian animals. The number has no doubt declined still further. The report also made the interesting observation that, in its attempts to meet the increased persecution, the animal had shown signs of retreating to moist lands and even changing its dietary habits. The blackbuck will remain the best champion of the beasts and birds of the open country, for, one hopes, surely the elegance of this Adonis must sooner or later put him in the minds of those whose responsibility it is to see that no more species of wild life in India go into oblivion.

The blackbuck's cousins, the chinkara or Indian gazelle (*Gazella gazella*), and the chousingha or fourhorned antelope (*Tetracerus quadricornis*), are similarly threatened. In 1964, in a letter to *The Field*, I gave the serious state of the little chousingha, accompanying it with a photograph I had a little while before taken of a female surprised in the act of being 'snapped', which might well be a rare picture as I have seen no other of a wild chousingha.

It is a small animal, about two feet high, and rarely seen in the tall grass and wooded hill slopes in which it generally lives. The chousingha had a wide distribution, but very little is known about its present status. Printed or typewritten literature on national parks and wild life sanctuaries assume its presence within their limits simply from its past range.

Chousingha is a Hindi word meaning 'four-horned'. The males alone carry horns, and are the only four-horned ruminants in the world. This alone lays a special claim for the continued survival of this antelope. The main pair of horns, about five inches long, are smooth, not ringed except sometimes at their bases, and lean very slightly forward at the tips. The front pair, situated between the eyes but a little above them, are variable in length, from about two and a half inches to mere knobs or skin callouses, or may even be altogether absent. Chousingha go about singly or in pairs, never in herds, which makes it difficult to see them even under good conditions. The reddish-brown coat can merge surprisingly well with lumps of all but very green grass. Although it is a pretty-looking animal and walks rather daintily on its toes, its running action is not smooth, with head thrust forward and the hind part, which is higher than its shoulder, going up in jerks. Whether one of these animals is with or without horns, it can be recognized by the line or stripe of darker-than-skin colour running down the front of each leg, more pronounced in the front ones.

The chousingha does not favour thick forest, preferring thorn scrub and ravines. But cultivation of a kind has extended to such tracts, and there are no observations to show that this antelope has taken to heavier cover.

The chinkara is about the same size as the chousingha, an attractive and graceful antelope. Its preferred habitat is also scrubland and thinly wooded ravines, and from both loss of habitat and falling a victim to weekend shooting, it has become scarce indeed. It was one of the casualties of the Tungabhadra dam-building. Formerly met with in small parties, it can seldom be seen now, and then only singly or in pairs. In many parts of the middle Deccan it is now thought to be extinct.

It would seem that the chinkara would have a greater chance of survival than the blackbuck as it is not so dependent on proximity of water, and also does not haunt the fringes of cultivated fields. On the other hand, they were never numerous. Dunbar Brander wrote, 'They can never be said to be numerous. Also they are often absent from tracts which have every appearance of suiting their requirements.'

Like the chousingha, the chinkara is included in the fauna of national parks and sanctuaries from old information. But I believe it has not gone to the extent of the other animal.

India's only ape, the hoolock or whitebrowed gibbon (*Hylobates hoolock*), found only in Assam within Indian limits but extending eastward into Burma and beyond, has been increasingly hunted by tribesmen in Assam in the changing forest scene of that State. The fur is used as part of the adornment of men and women, and the flesh is eaten by some tribes, as monkey flesh is eaten in parts of southern India.

The hoolocks' cries of '*whoop-poo!*', '*whoopoo!*', are one of the most cheerful of Indian jungle noises. It is a startling, loud, and piercing sound, and carries far, but after the first surprise, the cries are mirth-provoking. To see the hoolock walk is funny too. It walks erect, with its extraordinary long arms outstretched for balance, and is always in a flurry, not unlike a baby learning to walk and in a hurry to reach his mother's arms. The arms are very much longer than the legs (more than twice as long), and there is of course no tail. Standing up, it does not make three feet, but may give the impression of being taller because it is so very lanky.

It is an ape of the high trees, and consequently the lavish tree-felling in recent years has inevitably worked to its detriment. Hoolocks move about the tall tops of trees with the greatest abandon, swinging, walking, running, hanging, and eating in a whirl of arms and legs. The best time to see them is on a sunlit morning, when they love to display themselves, with hoots and cries, after a night spent in leafy shelters lower down. Their way of eating differs from the monkeys in that they do not gather their food—nut, fruit, grub, or insects—in handfuls, but pick it up in their fingers.

I believe a few have now been introduced into the Jaldapara

Sanctuary, just beyond the western limit of their range. This is a good move, as the unexploited interior of that sanctuary should suit them well. How precisely they are faring in Assam is not clearly known.

The golden or Gee's langur (*Presbytis geei*), discovered by Gee in 1953, was estimated by him in 1964 to number about 550 animals in all. The discovery of the only large unknown mammal on the Indian sub-continent in memory was appropriately made by one who did more than anyone else for the cause of wild life conservation in India, and to whom most turned on occasions when faced with wild life problems of national import.

It is a golden or light-chestnut-coloured monkey in winter, with the coat lightening to a creamy-white in the hot summer months. Its range is restricted to the Indo-Bhutan border between the Sankosh and Manas rivers, north of the Brahmaputra river, with just a possibility that a few may have infiltrated into the Khasi and Garo Hills, south of the river.

There are a number of other Indian monkeys, all of which fall into one or the other of two families, the langurs and the macaques. The two groups can be easily distinguished. The langurs are tall and lean with very long tails, the macaques squat and solid with short tails. The macaques also have cheek pouches to store food they cannot consume immediately.

The langur group comprises, besides the golden langur, three other monkeys—the Nilgiri langur, the common langur, and the capped langur. There are four in the macaque group—liontailed, Assamese, rhesus, and bonnet. I will now consider one from each group which is in considerable danger of extinction.

The Nilgiri langur (*Presbytis johni*), which I have very occasionally seen in the Nilgiri Hills and the forests of the Western Ghats, is a monkey on the danger list, although the latest news is not quite hopeless. It has a large 'paper' range all along the mid-Western Ghats down south to the Anaimalai and Palni Hills. It has been persecuted for its flesh, which seems to be eaten in the hill areas it inhabits. 'Extract of black monkey soup' is a well-known rejuvenating food-drink, and I have been offered hot monkey soup made from this extract more than once as I travelled in those parts, but had not the inclination to partake of it. I was assured that, apart from being a re-juvenant, it cured a great number of common ills like cold, influenza, flatulence, lassitude, low blood pressure, and so on. As with rhino horn, if the partaker of the soup was a believer, nothing anyone could say was of the least value. Perhaps, however, it makes a welcome, cheaply-come-by protein addition to the diet of the hill people, the jungle tribes particularly, who are often too poor to afford any meat except occasional goat meat. The handsome fur is also made into garments to keep out the cold of the hills in winter.

This langur is a fine-looking monkey, black-bodied, with a yellow-brown head and a long tail. The noisy cries of a troop as they forage for their food of fruit, berry, and nut, is a cheerful noise for the naturalist, just as they give them away to those on the hunt for them. They became so scarce a few years ago as to cause real concern, but for some reason I have not been able to discover, there seems to have been a slight revival lately.

Considerably worse off is the liontailed macaque (*Macaca silenus*), also a black-bodied monkey, but distinguished from the Nilgiri langur by its stockier build, big brown-grey ruff, and much shorter tail, and so contributing to the universal elixir, the extract of soup. This monkey has been through a disastrous period in recent years, and has rapidly disappeared in its range which is the same as that of the other. This is all the more mysterious, as it is a more secretive animal than the Nilgiri langur—unless the opening up of the forests of the Western Ghats has affected it more severely, for reasons that are not known. I once saw a troop which hugged the treetops, and later asked a possessor of the elixir in a nearby village how it was that they caught the monkeys who seemed so inaccessible. The answer was that it was a simple matter; the tree was cut down, and with it came the monkeys, who were killed off on the ground by clubbing or other means.

The slender loris (*Loris tardigradus*) was an animal familiar to me in south India, where I spent my boyhood. Like monkey men and bear men, there were others who carried around a loris or two and displayed them in street-corners, though, poor things, they could perform none of the tricks or acrobatics of

I

the monkey or the bear. Slow in movement, very docile, and staring-eyed, they were pathetic little creatures, hawked about in the heat and glare of the south. Nocturnal by nature, they must have suffered cruelly in the light, but the little boys who watched them, myself included, knew nothing of this. To amuse them and earn the smallest coins which were flung to its owner, the loris was made to climb sticks or to eat grasshoppers. All this is a thing of the past now, and though occasionally there is still a monkey man and very rarely a bear man, the loris man has wholly disappeared, and a very good thing too.

Curious as I was about animals even then, the men used to tell me how easy it was to catch a loris. They hid and waited at dusk, the hour when the loris came down a tree of the open jungles where it lived, or out of a cool crevice in the shrub, in search of food. A quick grab secured it, and it was duly transferred to a dirty bag. The loris of the streets was almost always in very poor condition, the soft and woolly fur clinging to it only in small patches or even totally gone.

The slender loris is a very rare animal now, of whose present fate little is known. There is another loris in India, the slow loris (*Nycticebus coucang*), of the far eastern forests, but of this I have no knowledge.

Few sportsmen have said a good word for the dhole, or Indian wild dog (*Cuon alpinus*). Indeed it is difficult to defend it, after one has read the accounts by hunters and naturalists of the pitiless method of its pack-hunting of sambar, chital, and other herbivores. I have, too, read notes of their treeing tigers and leopards, and attacking sloth bears, the majority of whom seem to have fled in complete defeat once set upon by the dogs in earnest.

There has been much sentimentality about the dangers of extinction faced by the herbivores on account of the dogs' hunting. If they were such a menace—their numbers were at no time great—the herbivores, for instance sambar and chital, should have been destroyed in the areas in which the dogs lived, and before a price was placed on the dogs' heads as vermin to be done away with wherever they were. More of a truth was that sportsmen did not like the emptying of their long-reserved shooting blocks as happened when a pack of dogs arrived. The dhole and the hoofed wild life had co-existed for centuries before man appeared on the forest scene as a potent factor, without the prey animals suffering losses from which they were unable to recover. I am, therefore, inclined to think that the part attributed to the dhole in the extermination of herbivores has been grossly overplayed.

There used to be a reward for every dhole killed, and there still is in many forests, quite unnecessarily, for now it is a scarce animal. Apart from such direct destruction, deforestation and the reduction of its natural prey have no doubt been the reasons for its disappearance.

But even the dhole has a claim for survival. It is a handsome animal, bright chestnut in colour, hard-muscled, and slim-waisted. It is quite easily distinguishable from the village pariah dog, or any other dog, or from its wild cousins, the wolf, the jackal, and the fox. It has its part to play in the balance of nature by killing off old and less able members of the deer tribe, although the toll may just as likely be levied on the fawns. The appearance of a dhole pack may drive deer to other parts of a forest, or even to other forests, but such a pack is not large and can consume only a certain amount of food. It is even possible that the dhole may have played a substantial part in keeping down excessive increase in deer, which might otherwise have consumed the vegetation and deteriorated in quality. A dhole pack does not attack human beings, and I have walked past and close to a pack in perfect safety. Their only reaction was to put up their heads and watch, and then show a tendency to make off.

Another much-maligned animal is the wolf (*Canis lupus*), and this too has all but finally gone from the plains. It is a creature of the scrubland, boulder-strewn hills with tussocks of grass, and village fringes, and after the discussion on the cheetah and the blackbuck, the reasons for its decline will be obvious. The wolf lived all over India, but as the plains went under the plough and the hoe, the bulldozer and the excavator, both itself and its natural prey, the antelopes, the hares, and other small plains mammals, had to go too.

With the scarcity in such prey, wolves took to killing domestic animals and, sadly in rare instances, children, this latter however being confined to certain areas in Uttar Pradesh. Although it is a result of a situation created by human agency, such kills receive wide publicity, as may be expected. Wolves driven to such rapacity through lack of food have of course to be killed, and killed they are by *shikaris*.

Wolves in India go about alone or in pairs, or very rarely in a small party, but never in such numbers as they were said to hunt in Russia. In the disappearance of such animals as the wolf, it is interesting to observe that man's interference with the equilibrium of wild life seems to get rid of the predators before the prey.

The sloth bear (*Melursus ursinus*) of India is unlike any other bear, and was the common bear of bear men in the streets of Indian cities and villages. Before about 1940, these men were commonplace. The animal was severely mutilated before it was safe to be trundled along, the claws being drawn, many of the teeth extracted, and the neck muscles debased with a tight collar. The elongated muzzle was tied tight with a rope, which was loosened only when the bear had to feed or drink. It was trained to do a variety of tricks—receiving fearful punishment during the breaking-in period—and beg for food. The long and shaggy hair, unkempt and bedraggled in nature, became even more so in the dust and grime of the towns. Bears must have suffered greatly in the torrid heat of day, as they were dragged from house to house, street to street, to repeat their repertoire of tricks, till their owner was satisfied with the day's earnings. These men have all but gone now, although an occasional one may suddenly make his appearance.

The sloth bear today is another vanishing animal. In places where it was common it is scarcely to be seen. Bear-hunting was a favourite sport with many sportsmen, and old sporting accounts are full of their exploits, legions of bear being slain sometimes in a single day in favoured areas, which were of jungle or scrub with rock-caves and boulder hideouts. Dunbar Brander wrote in his *Wild Animals in Central India* (1931):

The perusal of old books on sport, and the accounts of old shikaris, show that seventy or eighty years ago, bears, compared with modern conditions, occurred in almost incredible numbers, and in these days they were also found in country where they could be ridden and speared, and this was frequently done but is no longer a recognized method of hunting, chiefly by reason of the fact that they are no longer found in rideable country. Their decrease in numbers can be chiefly attributed to their being hunted by white men.

In addition to hunting by spearing, bears were sometimes pursued with a pack of dogs. This required a high degree of courage and skill from the hunter, and was considered very dangerous. Dunbar Brander tried this method himself.

The first occasion on which I attempted to spear a bear on foot with dogs I foolishly made a frontal attack, and the bear with a swift motion of the paw slipped the spear and got inside my guard. My next attempt although more successful, the spear getting home, only resulted in the shaft being broken, again by a sweep of the paw. On both occasions it was lucky for me the bear was already wounded and having profited by this experience under favourable circumstances, I never again attempted a frontal attack.

Sportsmen seeking less adventure wait for and shoot the bears as they become absorbed in eating fruit or sucking termites from anthills, of which latter they are extremely fond. Caution is required when seeking bear, because the terrain it favours is generally very much to its advantage. It is also one of the few animals in the Indian jungle which is liable to attack unprovoked, unless a sudden surprise encounter at close quarters can be classed as provocation, not because it is more aggressive and cross-tempered than other animals, but because it seems to get terribly confused when disturbed. It is unpredictable rather than bad, but for this reason I consider it the most dangerous animal for an unarmed man, such as I have always been, to encounter in the jungle. Numerous cases of unprovoked attack have been recorded, and the wounds inflicted are dreadful, as the bear prefers to attack the head and face. Villagers living in bear-inhabited territories have told me that this was the one animal they feared as they went about their daily tasks. F. W. Champion wrote in his *The Jungle in Sunlight and Shadow* (1934):

Unfortunately, however, the risk of an unexpected meeting with a short-tempered bear is a constant menace to forest officials and employees, and so many people have been mauled in recent years in the forests of Oudh that Government has been forced to place the large reward of Rs. 25 (nearly £2) on their heads.

The sloth bear has figured prominently in Indian folklore, and, interestingly, has been vested with human characteristics, perhaps more than any other animal. The reason for this—apart from the apparent unpleasant streak in its nature and its tendency to unprovoked attack—could very well be the fact that its paw-prints are very like human footprints, and its habit of standing up on its hind legs and looking about or letting fly with its paws, another human trait! But one can never tell if a bear is enraged from its expression, as it seems to have none behind the thick skin and fur of its face. Nor dies it lay back its ears or draw away its lips in a growl or a snarl.

The sloth bear is a greatly wandering animal, and with most of its kind killed off in rock and boulder country, its sole chance of survival appears to be in the sanctuaries, provided it keeps within them. This is, however, difficult for it to do, for it is ever on the move, an eater of fruit and berries of many kinds, and consequently a raider of orchards and gardens, and a seeker of variety in its diet. As against this, it has become virtually nocturnal, when formerly it was partly diurnal.

There are two other bears in India, the Himalayan black bear (*Selenarctos thibetanus*), in the lower levels of the Himalayas, and the brown bear (*Ursus arctos*), in the higher levels. The black bear is better known to the hill people, and is said to have an unpredictable temper like the sloth bear. Many cases of mauling have occurred. The brown bear is said to use the high altitude sanctuaries of Dachigam, Tons, and Rishiganga. Not much is known about the present status of either bear, but both are undoubtedly hunted for their fur.

The export of the red or lesser panda (*Ailurus fulgens*) from India is prohibited, and with good reason. It is believed to be nearly extinct in the part of its range in the Nepal and Sikkim Himalayas, with perhaps more survivors in the eastern part of its occurrence in upper Burma. From time to time, however, I have seen specimens in Calcutta's animal market, where they invariably died before they could be sold. Foreign zoos are not too keen to acquire them as they do not do well in captivity. Before the ban on their export, the former Calcutta animal dealer, George Munro, specialized in them, reared them successfully, and sold them to zoos oversea. They are apparently very susceptible to intestinal disorders, and also travel poorly.

The red panda is killed by tribesmen both for eating and for its fur. When intended for sale, it is caught by slipping a noose or slipknot on to a long bamboo and slipping it over its head while it is feeding. It lives largely in bamboo jungles, and so the apparatus for its capture can be made on the spot. It is also caught by shaking or scaring it off the tree or bush on which it may be lying, and grabbing it by the exceedingly long tail as it scampers on the ground for shelter. It is helpless when held dangling by the tail.

Hardly anything is known of the ways of these pandas, their breeding, and social habits. In captivity, they become very tame and make good pets. But domestication takes time, and in the meantime they can be resentful and pugnacious so that their handling requires care. Their claws are sharp, and non-retractile. An unusual characteristic is the soles of the paws, which are covered with hair. The red panda is a very attractive animal to look at, resembling both a cat and a bear. The white face is marked with a red stripe from above the eye to the gape, the body is reddish-brown or rust-coloured on the upper part, and the belly and legs are black, the black extending to the chin. The tail is also coloured like the upper body, with light ring markings. The panda is an almost unknown animal in most of India, and first achieved prominence when it appeared on a postage stamp some years ago.

The hill forests of its habitat are going through an unsettled time, and the animal falls an easy victim to marauding parties. Even if its killing by tribesmen for its flesh cannot be checked, at least the ban on its capture for export, and the export of its fur, can be enforced with strictness.

Porcupine quills were commonplace once, but most people today just do not know one when they see it. We generally have had a few in our house, collected by the boys on our jungle trips, and dangerously employed in lieu of rapiers in the numerous sword fights they have between themselves or with their friends in the best traditions of D'Artagnan or Cyrano de Bergerac. Both quills and their owners are fascinating parts of Indian jungle lore, and many are the stories told of the ferocity of the porcupine's attack when it shoots its quills at its attacker.

Tales apart, the quills are nothing more than modified hair. The Indian porcupine (*Hystrix indica*) is richly endowed with this modification, its neck, shoulders, and back being profusely covered with them, a literally bristling mantle of long and thin prickles overlaying an undergrowth of thicker and shorter quills. The quills are handsome-looking, and the shorter ones are ringed with alternate white-and-black bands, which are broad and do not merge into one another with any grey. The spines on the head are not as stiff as those on the back, where the longest ones are, these very long ones being all white and very dangerous. All spines are inclined rearward. At the tail end of the animal, the quills are not banded but are fully white and hollow and look like tiny wine-glasses with highly elongated bowls and without the bases. These are the so-called 'rattling quills', the rattle being more pronounced because of the hollow quills.

The quills can deal death to an unwary intruder provided the porcupine is sufficiently aroused. There have been many cases of tigers and leopards being grievously wounded by porcupines, some even dying on the spot with their heart and lungs pierced by the lethal spines. One of the chief causes of a tiger or a leopard turning man-eater is incapacitation from injuries sustained when attacking a porcupine or from an attack by an infuriated porcupine. A classic example was Jim Corbett's man-eating tigress of Muktesar. After he had shot her in an exciting encounter, he records:

> An hour later by the light of hand lanterns, and with a great crowd of men standing round, among whom were several sportsmen from Muktesar, I skinned the tigress. It was then that I found she was blind of one eye and that she had some fifty porcupine quills, varying in length from one to nine inches, embedded in the arm and under the pad of her right foreleg. Grievously wounded, incapacitated for life, and unable to kill her swift natural prey, the wretched tigress had taken to man-killing, and paid the penalty for her unnatural diet.

I have watched at leisure porcupines who have been annoyed for some reason. The erection of their quills, the tremendous extrusion of air from their nostrils, the rattling of their hollow tail quills, and the final launching backwards of the whole body is a very potent destructive process. This backward movement is a lightning-like affair, and any animal at its receiving end is likely to have a very thin time of it. It is not a question of the porcupine letting its quills fly but rather one of a simultaneous action in which the quills are thrust into the body of the would-be attacker and released by muscular movement. The quills are strong and steady enough to penetrate animal muscles, and when vital parts are punctured thus, the result is death. Otherwise, the quills are left in the flesh, and the wounded animal dies an agonizing death from wounds which suppurate and fester. Tigers and leopards succeed sometimes in pulling the quills off their flesh, but more often their frantic efforts result in the breaking of the quills close to the skin, which ensures that the quills remain in the flesh and incapacitate or kill the animal in the end.

The porcupine can let go its quills with impunity, as new ones grow quickly. No chance can be taken in approaching it, despite its innocent frontal look and general rotundity. It is capable of a lightning right-about turn, backing itself almost at the same time, and if an attack is intended it is pressed with quickness and determination. In the confusion following an attack when the injured animal is too bewildered to do anything, the porcupine makes a fast, shuffling getaway. The whole process has to be seen to be believed, so efficiently and quickly is it executed.

There are all kinds of superstitions about the porcupine, the kind depending on the district. Porcupines have a big range throughout the country, and are not partial to any one special type of habitat, though they generally favour a bush-and-boulder country, with plenty of little caves and crevices where they can make their homes. They are adept at digging and tunnelling, but I have not followed a tunnel to its conclusion, which is said to be a chamber in the earth.

Porcupines are hunted by tribesmen, particularly in central India, for their flesh, which is believed to endow the eaters with rare courage and a special ability to get out of danger, no doubt arising from the animals' own competence to defend themselves from the tiger and the leopard. The hunting is done by bow and arrow, but it is a hit-or-miss affair, as the arrow may easily clash with the bristling quills and not find the soft body of the rodent at all. Porcupines too are believed to carry reserve supplies of water in the hollow tail quills and they are credited with being excessively thirsty animals needing water at all times. This belief has sprung from a real-life observation, which is that these hollow quills do often fill with water as they cross shallow water in their paths quite readily.

Porcupines have decreased greatly with the disturbance to the forests, and shot for the fun of it by casual sportsmen, so that it is not easy to see them even in the Deccan jungles and such other areas where they were sure to be met with years ago.

The pangolin of India (*Manis crassicaudata*) is among the strangest-looking of all mammals. Covered with hard, strong scales except on the underside, the body resembles an outsize fir-cone, the immensely long and scaly tail tapering off from the body. The scaly tail provides an almost perfect protection from its enemies, the animal curling up into a ball and tucking its head and legs under cover of the tail. The scales are firmly attached to the body and cannot be detached by the attacking animal, and the pangolin is safe. The scale edges are sharp, and I have had my fingers cut badly trying to handle one.

It is a nocturnal animal, and feeds mainly on ants and insects. It spends the day curled up and hiding. A very good tree-climber, it uses its tail freely in the process of balancing and holding. To watch one dig can be diverting—as also to watch it eat ants and termites of which it is very fond. Both are lightning-like processes. One digging animal disappeared within minutes on what was pretty firm ground; but the earth yielded rapidly to the scythe-like action of the strong, curved claws of its fore-feet. Another amusing thing is to see a pangolin stand up on its hind legs and have a good look round.

Tribal people have now nearly exterminated it in the hill forests where it lives. The flesh is eaten, and is also unfortunately considered an aphrodisiac by some jungle tribes and as a fertility charm by others. Its scales are further made into ornaments which are believed to protect the wearer from all harm. It is a difficult matter to assess precisely its present status, but there is no doubt that it should receive total protection.

An animal which is familiar the world over for its playfulness and the stories that have been told about it is the otter. India too has her otters, three species of them: the common otter (*Lutra lutra*), the smooth otter (*Lutra perspicillata*), and the clawless otter (*Aonyx cinerea*). All of them must now be considered in danger of extinction. The chief reason for this seems to be the almost total disappearance of fish and other water life, which form the otter's main diet, in hill rivers and streams during the last fifteen years. Dynamiting or bombing of hill streams has been commonplace, killing off all life in long stretches of water and preventing re-establishment of life there. Otters also eat waterfowl and small rodents, but birds are difficult to catch and the supply of rodents in their habitats is not as plentiful as fish, crustacea, and frogs.

In the vicinity of villages, where there is always a certain amount of a miserable kind of fishing, the otter is looked upon as a rival consumer of fish and is killed on sight. The yield of village ponds and creeks is of the very lowest quality, but even so it forms some part of the villagers' food resources. Otter flesh is also eaten by certain low-caste people, who seem to consider it as something of a delicacy. Lairs are smoked out or set on fire, and the otters killed as they come pelting out for the safety of the nearest water.

Tales of its ferocity can be discounted, and are only told to justify its destruction. On the other hand, there have been many cases where otters have made excellent pets, safe enough for children to handle.

Otters probably survive in high-elevation streams in the Himalayas and Kashmir. These would be the common otter, a high-elevation creature which has practically gone from southern India's hill streams and lakes, and the clawless otter, a mid-level otter which has disappeared from the south and east of the country. Nothing has been seen of the smooth otter of plains waters for some time, and a few may survive in remote pockets.

The ratel, or honey badger (*Mellivora capensis*), has a 'paper' range all over India, and has lived its life adapting it to many types of forest and plain, where food of one kind or another was available—small mammals, birds, reptiles, and insects. It has been said by all who have known the jungle, naturalists and others, to be the most courageous little beast of the Indian jungle, and they have in support given instances of it putting animals many times its size to flight, including the lord of them all, the tiger. Dunbar Brander wrote, 'Considering their size, they are endowed with a courage possessed by no other animal'.

Its main offensive armaments are its powerful claws, sharp teeth, and stink glands. Its thick hide, loose and covered with coarse, stiff hair, with a heavy layer of fat beneath, and quick movements, protect it from its foes. It is a great raider of bees' nests, and apparently enjoys full immunity to the stings of the infuriated bees.

Its fearlessness is a byword in the history of the Indian jungle. It was never much to be met with, and is hardly to be seen at all now.

There was a solitary specimen in the Alipore Zoo, Calcutta, for many years. It was a particular favourite with our sons. Then, suddenly, one day in 1965, it was not there. Dead and gone, it left behind a much-mourned cage.

Gee made a survey in 1962 of the Indian wild ass (*Equus hemionus*) and arrived at a figure of 870 animals. Only one previous attempt had been made to find their number, by Sálim Ali in 1946, and he thought there were 3,000 to 5,000 of them left then. All other 'estimates' were only guesses, and ran well into several thousands. Gee's survey showed that there had been a serious decline in their fortunes.

The main habitat of this ass was the Rann of Cutch, in western India, where it received protection from the rulers of Cutch, but it also lived in the arid areas of north-west India, whence it has wholly gone now. It survives mainly in the Little Rann of Cutch (there is a Great Rann), and Gee put all but ten stray animals as being concentrated there. The Little Rann is an area of about a thousand square miles and is a salt-impregnated flat waste, and only a couple of feet above sea-level. It is dry in winter and covered with water in the monsoon months with rain water and water from the sea blown over by the strong winds.

Persecution in the past was mainly from sportsmen who speared it after a chase, and animal-catchers who ran it down and caught it by noose for zoos or for breeding mules. The local people themselves, however, did not molest them, and still do not do so, being vegetarians and content to drive away the asses if they came to raid their crops.

In recent years, however, threats to their survival have come from two directions. The region has been a combat area between India and Pakistan, and it seems certain, from area reports, that the troops took pot-shots at the asses for target practice in their idle hours. Then, reclamation-cultivation projects of parts of the marshlands have been in progress, and more are proposed. These will inevitably reduce the extent of their habitat, and facilitate shooting from their operational centres.

Additionally, the ass is also liable to loss from disease, and numbers died from a blood infection called *surra* in 1958 and from an epidemic of South African Horse Sickness in 1961.

One of the most beautiful of India's creatures is the Indian giant squirrel, sometimes called the Malabar squirrel (*Ratufa indica*). This squirrel lives mainly in the semi-deciduous forests of the country, atop the high trees, where it spends practically all its time. Like its more familiar and smaller cousins, the striped squirrels, it is a born acrobat. I have watched its fantastic leaps from the top of one slender tree to the top of another, and when a crash seemed inevitable and imminent, the little beast had landed on a frail branch, clung to it, transferred itself to a heavier branch capable of bearing its weight, and fled into the green interior of the tree. On one occasion, measuring on the ground between the trees, I found one of the squirrels had leapt a clear twenty-five feet, a most imposing performance! When it flings itself thus aerially, it looks much like a museum specimen spreadeagled for study, but for the waving hair of the great, furry tail with its white tip. As the squirrel moves restlessly and in lightning-quick movements, the tail is constantly doing its work of balancing, holding, and generally acting as a safety limb to the animal. To watch it needs patience, as it is liable to disappear quickly at the first sign of danger. But when it believes itself undiscovered, it may lie flat along a branch without knowing that its hanging tail, swaying in the breeze, is wholly giving it away.

This squirrel is killed in the Malabar area in the State of Kerala for its flesh, and indeed all squirrel meat is eaten in village areas in and around forests. It is not as common as it was, and I was told that when tree-felling takes place, numbers of the squirrels are killed on the ground. It seems quite likely that they have declined seriously, because one can no longer see their round nests of twigs and leaves except occasionally, whereas they used to be plentiful twenty years ago in the forests of their habitat. The lovely red-brown and long-tailed little animal was one of the joys of the mixed deciduous forests, a joy for which one has to search for long now.

There are many other animals which have so severely decreased in their native ranges—either because their own particular types of habitat have gone or because of direct human persecution following disturbances to the habitat—that they may be considered to be in much danger of total extermination. Of many of them I have very little or no personal knowledge—beasts like the bharal and the shapu, wild sheep of the high altitudes; the Himalayan and Nilgiri tahrs, in the far north and the far south, with the southern animal estimated at no more than 400 head in a census taken by the Nilgiri Wild Life Association in 1963; the ibex and the markhor, of the splendid scimitar and the spiralled horns so beloved of old-time sportsmen; the three goat-antelopes, takin, serow, and goral, also of high elevations; the snow leopard, despoiled for its lovely fur; the smaller members of the cat family, the golden cat, the fishing cat, the leopard cat, and the marbled cat, all beautiful; members of the civet group; the crabeating mongoose, largest of the mongooses; the pygmy hog and the hispid hare, both now feared extinct; and many, many others, big and small.

The sub-continent of India provides an astonishing variation of habitats for wild life, and consequently has an amazingly varied animal and bird life in its 1·8 million square miles. There are the thick, evergreen and rainswept forests of Assam and south-west India, the snow-covered Himalayan regions with the dense tropical forests and swamps of the foothills and lower valleys, the open grasslands and scrub jungles of the Deccan plateau, the dry and arid lands of Rajasthan, the great teak and *sal* forests of Madhya Pradesh, the mangrove swamps of the Sunderbans, the thorn jungles and desert wastes of Gujerat and Cutch, and many other intermediate habitats besides. In these still live a great variety of mammals, birds, and reptiles, most of them unknown to the common man or only remotely heard of. Many out of this astonishing array of wild life are in the course of being exterminated for ever.

VI

THE DEER TRIBE

As the dawn was breaking the sambar belled—Once, twice
and again!

RUDYARD KIPLING

INDIA IS PROUDLY REPRESENTED in her deer family. It ranges
from the largest of them, the sambar, to the tiny mouse deer,
through an astonishing range of sizes represented by the
barasingha or swamp deer, the hangul or Kashmir stag (also
sometimes called barasingha), the thamin or browantlered
deer, the chital or spotted deer, the muntjac or barking deer,
the hog deer, and the musk deer. An adult sambar stag stands
nearly five feet at the shoulder and weighs up to 700 pounds,
while the little mouse deer is only a foot high and weighs only
a few pounds.

I had an unusual encounter once with a sambar stag in an
open forest in southern Uttar Pradesh, some miles from the
holy city of Varanasi. The forest held a few sambar, some chital
and chinkara. It was a beautiful day, not winter yet, but already
cool. I was on foot and alone, and weaving in and out of the
light brush which was all there was between the trees which
were dotted about as in a parkland. I saw chital and chinkara in
ones and twos, but they hurried along in light bounds and
scampers. Suddenly, I saw a most magnificent sambar stag. I
was now in somewhat heavier undergrowth and, taking advantage of the cover, I began to stalk him. I lost him for a few
moments, but when I stepped out of the brush into a clearing,
he did the same from its opposite side. The clearing was roughly
circular, and about twenty-five feet across. I stopped, and he did
too, and stood majestically with his great antlers held high,
watching me. I was surprised that he did not turn round and

go, and as there was no point in pretending I was not there, I kept very still. The sambar showed no sign of agitation. I now began to move forward, in a straight line towards him, only very little at a time, meanwhile slowly bringing up my camera, which hung from my neck in a gentle, continuous movement from below the waist.

I expected the stag to turn and go off any moment, but to my amazement, he moved not at all but simply stood there staring. In late years I had discovered that animals were attracted to me, without my knowing anything about it—all kinds of animals—and the thought now came to me that the sambar too was perhaps similarly affected. Then an even more unexpected thing happened. Presently, he too began to step forward, a little at a time. In a few minutes we were within about five feet of each other. I had also begun to take his pictures, but he was in no wise disturbed. It was an extraordinary situation. I could now have taken a step forward, extended my arm, and touched him. I had been unexcited till then, but now for some reason I became unsure of what the sambar might do. There was certainly an element of fear in the feeling. In all my years in the jungle, I have never been afraid of being killed—this may sound boastful, but it is perfectly true—but have been afraid of being left with a serious injury or a lost limb. It may be that the change of mood in me communicated itself to the stag. But it seemed that, at the same instant, he turned and began to walk slowly away into the trees. The incident had a miserable sequel. The precious roll of film inexplicably fell out of its cassette on the following day as I was reloading the camera in another forest, and was ruined.

The sambar (*Cervus unicolor*) was widely distributed all over India where there were fair stretches of forest but, as with other wild life, it has now disappeared or thinned in many parts following heavy loss of habitat and intensified poaching. The fully adult stag is a grand-looking animal, with a coat turned almost black from brown, often a mane about the neck and throat, and antlers which have taped fifty inches or more, although forty inches should be reckoned an exceptionally good head today. The horn quality is judged not only by the length but also by weight and thickness. I am not able to speak with any certainty of the period of year when sambar shed their

K

antlers, but I have seen more cast-off antlers in March–April than at any other time. The horns soon begin to grow again and are clear of velvet in about six months. Many times I have seen sambar bleeding freely from the velvet as a result of minor injuries or scrapings, as the growing horn is encased in thick and soft skin filled with tiny blood-vessels and is very sensitive during the early period of its growth. If one watches a stag in velvet long enough, there is a marked difference in behaviour then and when he is in full horn. In the latter case, he uses his horn freely, crashing his way through trees, but when in velvet he is very careful to avoid thick forest where it might get entangled in the branches and be damaged. If a fight is unavoidable with another stag, the animal, which would have made full use of its horns normally, holds them back and uses his forefeet instead.

Shed sambar horns are seldom intact as, if porcupines are present as they generally are in sambar forests, they gnaw them and make short work of them so that they soon disappear. Much more study is needed on the whole process of horn growth and shedding, before its mysteries can be known. Various theories have been expounded by sportsmen based on their own observations, often confined to a particular geographical area, and there may be many things about the process which we do not know. For example, it has been observed that in one area the stags do not shed their horns every year. In another, a stag in velvet was shot as late as in December. Freak horns have been found dropped in the forests, but the reasons for growing such horns are not known. Food available in particular forests may also have an effect on horn growth.

The sambar stag is quite a sultan in the rut, but not as many-wived as the blackbuck. Sambar numbers have of course never been anything like the blackbuck's, and the stag has therefore to be content with a few hinds. But he fights savagely for their possession. After the rut, the big stags wander about on their own, but sometimes two can be seen together.

Sambar is the cleverest of all Indian deer, and acts in a number of ways to avoid detection and to escape from both its natural enemies and man. In former days, when sportsmen, by and large, observed the laws and ethics of hunting, the sambar had an excellent chance of escape, as the commonly accepted method of hunting sambar was by stalking. This skill of the hunter, matched against the skill of the sambar in concealing itself and making a good getaway in a favourable situation, gave the animal an even chance of survival. The essence of stalking was to discover the animal before it became aware of the hunter's presence. This was no mean feat even for an experienced sportsman. Moreover, a sportsman went only after an adult stag with shootable horns, and so had first to find such an animal, and then to stalk it unseen. But today the vast bulk of the hunting is done from a jeep, with spotlight and rifle with telescopic sights, and the size and sex of the quarry does not matter. The sambar has made a large and prominent target for these hunters in the denuded forests of today, and fallen an easy victim. Most terrible of all, numbers of wounded animals are left behind to die a slow and agonizing death. Seldom does a hunter of today follow up a wounded beast to put it out of its misery, for not only is it quite beyond his ability, but also he does not care.

Sambar is also slain by the villagers with their ancient firearms or caught in wickedly potent snares and despatched. This deer is unfortunately fond of feeding off the grain of growing crops, and as they come stealing to the cultivated fields at night, they stumble and fall into pits or step into snares, all ready and prepared for their reception. It is hard to pass judgement on the villager who is chronically short of meat, or, for that matter, often of any food. But this of course does not help the sambar, carrying as it does plenty of meat. The flesh is coarse, but welcome all the same, and the skin too is valuable as it can be turned into good leather and put to many uses. The deer is aware of the persecution, because in late years it has become more or less wholly nocturnal, retiring into the cover of trees at an early hour in the morning and reappearing only after sunset.

Near camp areas in the sanctuaries, sambar can, however, be seen in the day, as they are free from molestation. The finest herd I ever saw was one of twelve animals in Kaziranga, and as I was seated on my elephant, the entire herd marched past in my front, across a small strip of water, in single file, quite unafraid. In Periyar, I once saw a very splendid sight of a great sambar stag outlined on a rise with the setting sun behind him.

The wild dog used to be an important enemy of the sambar, but with its general disappearance it is no longer important. I once saw an unusual sight in Bihar, of a sambar hind being hunted by a pack of village pariah dogs. The scene as I came upon it was one in which the hind was taking its stand in a little mudpool, flanks heaving and facing the dog pack. It was apparent she had run a long way. The dogs were without doubt village curs, not wild dogs. They were tremendously excited, and yapping, but did not enter the water. It struck me that they were a pack of dogs which were no amateurs at the game. Clearly they belonged to poachers who had trained them to run down deer. They were on their own then, but following a pattern. In a few moments, the sambar wheeled round and bounded out of the pool, only to be pursued once again by the wretched pack. I hoped she would escape.

Sambar are prone to epidemic diseases, caught from infected cattle, and are decimated by such attacks. The breeding rate also is slow. If too many die out or are killed off in any area, the stock just does not recover but is slowly extinguished. The sharp, deep alarm call of the sambar, 'dhank', 'dhank', is one of the thrilling sounds of the Indian jungle, as it may presage the near-presence of a tiger or a leopard. When one hears it, therefore, there is a double anticipatory excitement—of seeing a fine stag and a big cat.

At the other end of the scale in size is the mouse deer, also called the Indian chevrotain (*Tragulus meminna*). This is not a true deer at all, taxonomically speaking, as it belongs to a separate group of ruminants, a group made up of two Asian and one African chevrotains. It is a pretty little creature of slender legs and high hindquarters, with tiny tusk-like canines which are quite harmless and used only in fighting between themselves.

The mouse deer has been mercilessly killed off in most of its range in southern India. The High Ranges where it was once abundant in the deciduous forests have now none of this little animal left in them. I have searched for them there. At one of the plantations my fear was confirmed, and my hosts said that both the gaur (great gaur heads adorn bungalows and club-houses in this district) and the mouse deer became extinct some years previously. The Indian planters who had succeeded their British predecessors were responsible, and, of course, the local *shikaris*. These planting men, like many of those I met in north-east India, were not planters at heart at all, but had drifted into the plantation business in the expectation of making big money quickly, or filled well-paid jobs through influence and connections. They have little idea that such heavy slaying of wild life must eventually lead to its total extermination, and some even advanced the argument that, if that did happen, they would have had their fun and their successors would have to find something equally diverting to amuse themselves. To views such as these there could be no answer.

Mouse deer meat is highly rated in the villages, and in the troubled political situation in that State of the past many years, there was no safeguard for the animals in the forests outside the Periyar Sanctuary. Mouse deer probably now survive chiefly in the Nilgiri Hills, where they have been observed to have retreated into brush and secondary forest as the primary forests have been felled or opened up. Also, they have become crepuscular, or even nocturnal, as a result of the persecution.

The musk deer (*Moschus moschiferus*), which is about twice as big as the mouse deer—which still makes it a small animal—is yet another on the brink of extinction, at least within Indian limits. Whether it survives in any numbers in the mountain fastnesses north of India is unknown.

It is an animal of special interest, as it is an intermediate type between the deer and the antelopes. The musk gland under its abdomen is of course its speciality, while another characteristic feature is the well-developed canine teeth in the males. The musk of Eastern commerce is, perhaps, not as familiar an item today as it used to be, but musk is still used for making scents and is also sold as a stimulant.

There is no captive specimen in any of the Indian zoos. The protection of this deer is a rather hopeless proposition, even in the high-altitude sanctuaries of Rishiganga and Tons, where there is no surveillance whatever. In both, the animal has, however, been seen.

The prettiest of all Indian deer is also the best known, the chital or spotted deer (*Axis axis*). This is one species of deer which still lives in good numbers, not in thousands as was the case, but in good herds of twenty to fifty animals, which is quite exceptional in the conditions of today. But an experienced sportsman put their numbers at no more than five per cent of their strength in the 1940s.

They occur in all forests where there is cover, good grazing, and a good supply of water within easy reach. They have been sleek or scrawny according to local conditions, and the poorest wild specimens were perhaps those I saw in a thorn jungle in Jamnagar, south of the Gulf of Cutch. There was little true green vegetation, and lantana barred the way everywhere. Fat, sleek animals have occurred in the Kumaon Hills and other Uttar Pradesh forests, the great *sal* forests of Madhya Pradesh, the Godavari valley, and other tracts endowed with luscious glades and water-full streams.

Chital are fond of cultivated crops, and so near the proximity of villages many pay the price by getting shot or maimed in snares and pits. By virtue of their numbers, chital are also the main sufferers in the occasional mass-hunting by tribesmen which still takes place in remote parts of India. I have said before that the danger to wild life from tribal hunters is nothing like what it is in East Africa, nor is such mass-hunting as common or as widespread. But it does exist in isolated areas. Such a one is the Ayodhya Hills in the Purulia district in Bihar, where forests are annually burnt to celebrate the festival of *Baisakhi Purnima*. Several thousand tribesmen and women, armed with bows and arrows and antiquated firearms, set fire to the forests in a large circle. As the animals rush out at the only exit, they are tripped in snares and slaughtered without regard to size or sex. Both forests and wild life are destroyed, but there is no interference from the authorities as the whole thing is considered an old tribal custom. It may be so, but the practice must have surely originated when the tribesmen were heavily dependent on hunting as a mode of living. They are not now, having taken to various other occupations, but the annual holocaust goes on just the same.

As in the case of the sambar, information on the shedding and growing of antlers is inconclusive. Individual accounts may be reliable, but they are applicable to particular territories only. The time of year when chital antlers are shed has long been debated in sporting literature. Some sportsmen have thought that they are dropped throughout the year, while others have held the view that the shedding occurred at particular seasons. Data are available in support of both theses. My own scattered observations incline me to support the first theory, but until such time as studies are made systematically in all parts of India—an unlikely event—whether a definite pattern exists must remain a matter of conjecture.

Chital are the first target of casual sportsmen, as they are usually seen more often and in more numbers than any other wild life. Still, because of their past plenty, they hold on in many forest areas where all else is gone. Unfortunately, one only too often comes across maimed or injured animals, and there is nothing more pathetic than an incapacitated chital stag. It is one of nature's noblest creatures, of eye-filling beauty and joy, and the spotted and sheen-glossed hide, the lovely spreading antlers, and eyes ringed with natural kohl, are not things easily forgotten.

I shall for ever remember the magnificent stag in Bandipur Sanctuary whose antlers were caught in the lower branches of a tree, as I approached the herd of which he was undoubted lord and master. As I came near, his struggles became frantic as he tried to free himself and join his large harem, which had speedily scuttled away. I stopped and stayed very still, so as not to alarm him further, and I was afraid he might injure himself if he went on much longer. The tawny, white-dappled body twisted and turned. At last, the antlers broke free, and with a great and splendid bound the stag was away, no doubt to chastise his does who had left him to his fate.

There was a deer in the Chumbi valley of Tibet, which drives a wedge between Nepal and Sikkim and is just outside the Indian border, which is now very probably extinct. It was the shou, or Sikkim stag (*Cervus elaphus wallichi*), and it very occasionally penetrated into India, but, whether for that reason or any other, it has generally been considered part of the wild life of the sub-continent.

In addition to the Chumbi valley, the shou also lived in the wooded valley of the Tsangpo, as the river Brahmaputra is known in Tibet, to the east of Lhasa, and in north Bhutan, but not in Sikkim itself, though it is called the Sikkim stag. It is a species of red deer, larger even than the majestic hangul, or Kashmir stag, from which it is distinguished by the shape of its antlers.

In the summer of 1962, I was in Kalimpong, the Indo-Sikkimese border town in the Himalayan foothills which was so much in the news during the conflict with China, and came across a piece of information on this deer which threw some light on its fate. I saw two left antlers which looked suspiciously like the shou's, one on either side of the main doorway of the Himalayan Hotel, which is owned and run now by the descendants of David Macdonald (he was alive then, aged 89), who was British Trade Agent in Tibet from 1909 to 1925 and stationed in the Chumbi valley for many years.

My story is of a stag shot in the Chumbi valley in 1920 or 1921, and believed at that time to be the last in that region. It was told to me by Mrs. Anne Perry, eldest of Macdonald's daughters. The stag was shot by a Col. Renwick of the Remounts at Lingmathang. Mrs. Perry was not quite certain if it was in 1920 or 1921, but it was about a year before her marriage in 1922. She went and saw the stag after it had been shot and, as far as she knew, the skin and antlers were sent to the Natural History Museum in London. It was agreed by everyone at that time that the animal was the 'last' shou in the Chumbi valley.

On my return to Calcutta after that visit, I tried to find all written references to the shou in the present century, and there were very few indeed. R. Lydekker in his *Game Animals of India* (1924) wrote that the shou was not found in Nepal or Sikkim, and that its main habitat was the Chumbi valley, extending into Bhutan. He quoted from a letter to *The Field* of 27 October 1906, written by Lt.-Col. H. A. Iggulden:

My own observations and enquiries on this matter may be of interest to naturalists, for whilst in Tibet with the military expedition of 1903–1904 I made enquiries regarding the stag, and saw a considerable number of skulls and horns at various places between our boundary on the Talep Pass and Lhasa. I came to the conclusion that these deer are not found to the west of a line drawn north and south between Shigatse and the northern part of Sikkim. They are never found in Sikkim itself, as the climate there is too damp, though one or two may possibly at times have crossed the boundary. There are a fair number in the Chumbi and branch valleys, which are well wooded, though they are probably more plentiful in some of the northern Bhutanese valleys. After leaving the Chumbi valley these deer are not again encountered until the Tsangpo or Brahmaputra Valley is reached, where there are some herds of them in a valley to the north of the Kamba Pass, which were said to be protected by the Dalai Lama, and were completely unmolested. They also inhabit the high mountains on both sides of the Brahmaputra for many miles to the east, probably as far as the unexplored Brahmaputra Falls. I next definitely heard of their existing in the bare hills to the north-east of Lhasa, and was told that they were occasionally seen and killed some few miles from that city.

Mrs. Perry's account seemed to tie up with a note by Col. F. M. Bailey quoted by R. I. Pocock in an article which appeared in the *Journal of the Bombay Natural History* in 1942:

Shous used to be fairly common on the ridge east of the Chumbi Valley between that valley and Bhutan. East of this there used to be some in Bhutan. They lived, I think, in Bhutan but came over the ridge into the Chumbi Valley in the summer and autumn. About November and December the Chumbi Valley people cut fuel for their winter supply. Deep snow does not usually come till later. This disturbs the forest and drives the deer back into Bhutan. In the summer of 1921 I saw two hinds and a young one above Lingmotang[1] in the Chumbi Valley. There must have been very few left and I believe all were exterminated a few years ago, as I am told there are none in this part of Bhutan now. I saw a few in the district of Tsari. Here the shou will be more or less artificially preserved for a long time I hope, as the place is very holy and no life may be taken there.

In the book *Sport and Travel in the Highlands of Tibet* (1927), a narrative of the journey of the authors, Sir Henry Hayden and Cesar Cossar, through Tibet in 1922, Hayden describes their stalk of a herd of eleven shous—all they saw of the deer during

[1]Obviously the same as Mrs. Perry's 'Lingmathang'.

many attempts to find it in its reputed haunts—in a valley off the Tsangpo. Cossar shot one of them, which he thought was a male, but it turned out to be a hind. 'It was a fine beast, bigger than a red deer, and in very good condition.' The two men saw no shou in the Chumbi valley.

Then, in a note written to the *Journal of the Bombay Natural History Society* in 1959, F. Ludlow summarized his experience of the shou as he had visited all the areas in which it was said to occur, although his travels had taken place some years previously. According to him, the shou had not lived in the western parts of Tibet in recent times. Writing of the Chumbi valley, he said:

> When I was in Gyantse from 1923 to 1926, a few shou inhabited the Chumbi Valley in the vicinity of a little plain called Lingmothang. In the winter of 1925 I saw three hinds in this area, but no stags. The shou was also reported to occur at this time in the upper reaches of the Ha Valley in Bhutan, but even at this early date the animal was said to be on the verge of extinction, and in later years Raja Dorje, who owned the Ha Valley, told me he was convinced that all had been exterminated. In 1933 and 1949, in company with Major G. Sheriff I traversed Bhutan from west to east keeping for the most part to the temperate zone under the curves of the Great Himalayan Range. Burhel were plentiful, also musk deer and barking deer, and in certain valleys takin, but I saw no shou nor did I hear of any, though the country seemed eminently suited to their needs.

Of south-eastern Tibet and the Lhasa area, Ludlow wrote that there were no shou although he travelled there extensively, except in Tsari, where some deer were left as it was a holy place. Even here the shou were harassed and killed from time to time by animist tribesmen who raided from other areas. Ludlow's servant had seen shou in the Reting district north of Lhasa, which was corroborated by Lhasa officials, and the shou received protection from the lama of high rank of the area.

Even if the shou was not totally extinct before the Chinese occupation of Tibet, it is very doubtful if it has survived the massive events of the last ten years. The Chinese have long held a belief that the horns of deer in velvet possess aphrodisiac qualities, and, as we have seen with rhino, this is a powerful motivation for killing. The Chinese concentrated in strength in the autumn of 1962 in the Chumbi valley before the invasion of India, and are still there in large numbers. Further, they have no religious scruples, and the immunity enjoyed by the shou in parts of its old range from this reason must have been destroyed long ago. In short, unless there is reliable evidence to the contrary, it may be assumed that this fine deer is extinct. Other vanishing deer have been saved from extinction by raising captive herds, but it would seem that even this is too late for the shou.

The rare and beautiful browantlered deer (*Cervus eldi*), or thamin, which was declared extinct in 1951 survives in a floating swamp in the former Princely State of Manipur, between Assam and East Pakistan. In a survey made in 1960, Gee estimated its number at about a hundred animals. I have only seen specimens in the Alipore Zoo in Calcutta, and the deer derives its name from the brow tines which come straight out in a forward sweep, and form almost semi-circles with the beams in a continuous curve. Another characteristic is the unusual development of the hind pasterns which are horny and without hair and make ample contact with the ground, well suited to progression in swamp and marsh country. There are sub-species of this deer in Burma, Thailand, and Indo-China, but the Indian animals are found only in the Keibul Lamjao swamps of Logtak Lake in Manipur. Known as *sangai* to the local people, the deer were protected by the Princely Government from 1934, but in 1951 it was thought that they had died out, and so it was announced. Apparently, however, a few had retreated into the heart of the swamp where, upon their rediscovery, a sanctuary was created in 1954 for their total protection. The approach to the inner swamps can be made only by boat and that by painfully pushing through a vast mat of humus and dead vegetation. To this the deer owe their survival.

As may be imagined, not a great deal is known about this deer. Preservation in Keibul Lamjao should not present too great a problem, as all that needs to be done is to leave the animals well alone in the swamps, which are sufficiently inaccessible, and take steps to see that they are not even occasionally molested by the local residents. For visitors, the remoteness of the habitat is a disadvantage, but the sanctuary has not really much tourist potential, as few people take enough interest in wild life to travel a long way just to see one species of deer.

The barking deer or muntjac (*Muntiacus muntjak*) and the hog deer (*Axis porcinus*) are two smaller but well-known members of India's deer tribe. Both have been severely affected by loss of big stretches of habitat, and by poaching. Neither is easy to see today, as not only are their numbers reduced, but they move about singly or in pairs, although barking deer may occasionally make a small party. I have seen barking deer in most forests of India, and hog deer less often, mainly in the grass jungles of northern India. Both fall prey to a variety of predators, from the tiger to the wild dog and the python. Theirs is a hard life, ever on the watch for enemies, but their survival will not depend on whether they will escape their enemies, but whether man will leave them with enough habitat to live in and stop his persistent pursuit for their meat or for his amusement. Hog deer are particularly affected by loss of habitat, as they prefer grass jungles near water, and it is this kind of land which is favoured for taking over for cultivation. Barking deer suffer much in dam projects, when their favourite haunts of wooded hills and ravines are destroyed.

One of the most familiar jungle sounds is the alarm call of the barking deer, a hoarse call repeated at short intervals. To see one of these deer nibbling at foliage is one of nature's prettiest sights. It is said that it is not beyond eating meat occasionally. I once saw a stag at an old kill, a tiger's or leopard's, but, as it fled, I did not actually see it feeding. The stag cannot be approached without caution, as its long upper tusks can, in a rush, inflict serious injury. It seldom uses, for offensive purposes, its small hooked antlers, which consist of a brow tine and an unbranched beam.

The young hog deer are spotted, and have sometimes been mistaken for the young of chital. But the adults are squat-looking and have none of the chital's grace.

Both deer survive in a number of sanctuaries and are in no immediate danger, while steadily declining in numbers.

Not unlike the browantlered deer at Keibul Lamjao, surviving hangul (*Cervus elaphus hanglu*), or Kashmir stag, are concentrated in a small sanctuary, Dachigam, in Kashmir. The hangul, like the shou, is also a kind of red deer, and received a measure of protection from the rulers of Kashmir. The present sanctuary was formerly their private shooting preserve, and shooting was restricted to themselves and their guests. Gee estimated that fifty years ago as many as 5,000 hangul may have lived there and in the surrounding forests. Numbers decreased as with all other wild life till about the Kashmir troubles, when it was thought that there were no more than a thousand left. But from then on, as the combat areas extended, and with considerably less law and order, hangul, black bear, and pig were all being killed off. Official figures continued to be optimistic, till Gee's surveys put the number of hangul at 250 in 1960, and as few as 180 in 1965.

The hangul lives in wooded hills, and goes about in small parties. It spends the summer in Upper Dachigam at 12,000 feet, and comes down to Lower Dachigam at 6,000 feet in the winter. The antlers are shed before the deer start going up again, and when they descend to the lower levels the following winter, they are in hard horn again. If the winter is excessively severe, the hangul may descend to still lower levels, but it then runs a great danger from the poacher, who is never far away or without work even in the sanctuary.

Other dangers to this deer are the continuous decline of its grassland range from overgrazing by domestic livestock, of which there are thousands in the tract. Grazing animals further carry disease into the sanctuary and easily infect the deer. Danger from predators, the occasional black bear or leopard, should be small, with the enormous supply of domestic animals. But some deaths have occurred in fawns and young deer, while the adult stags seem to be left well alone.

Last, but by no means the least, is the beautiful swamp deer, or barasingha (*Cervus duvauceli*). It is an exclusively Indian animal, except for a few specimens on the Nepalese side of northern Uttar Pradesh. Another name used for the deer is the 'gond', but the hangul is also sometimes called 'barasingha' in Kashmir. Two races are said to exist, those which live primarily in swamp forests, as in parts along the base Himalayan foothills in Uttar Pradesh, West Bengal, and Assam—and in the Sunderbans if there are any left there, which I doubt—and those which live in the great forests of the interior, as in Madhya Pradesh, where the ground is firm. It is said that the hooves of the northern deer are splayed to suit the swamp habitat, but I have not examined enough numbers of hooves of either group to have formed an opinion. But the splayed hooves may well be so, as a result of adaptation to habitat.

Swamp deer have become extremely shy in late years and are very difficult to approach, a result of human persecution. Particularly in the *terai* areas of Uttar Pradesh and in north-east India, their killing by casual sportsmen has been great. The deer, previously day-feeding, have become partly nocturnal. The shooting of this deer is facilitated by the fact that they are gregarious at all times, and in the rutting season a master stag may have as many as twenty hinds in his harem. I have heard of cases where the jeep sportsmen have merely opened fire on a herd, without taking particular aim at one beast, and left behind a few dead but more severely injured animals. This was in the *terai* of Uttar Pradesh, but it might have happened anywhere.

Even in Kanha National Park, which is justly famous for its swamp deer, the numbers have fallen from about 660 in 1935 and 550 in 1953, to about a mere 200 now. A very poor count indeed, considering that the tract, as the Banjar Valley Reserve, once teemed with this deer. When I first went to the Park in 1961, I had been told that the animals there were not shy at all. But the reverse was the case. Swamp deer were particularly difficult. It seemed that they were very much on edge, no doubt after persistent harassment from poachers. George B. Schaller gives in his *The Deer and the Tiger* (1967), a classic work, disease as an additional cause for the decline, by which the young are aborted.

I remember that trip as a very disappointing one. Despite prolonged correspondence and promises of arrangements made, when I arrived at the main camp on a bitterly cold December night, everything was shut and barred and there was no staff around to be seen. It was a long time before I could get one of the resthouses opened for me, and then I myself collected dry wood and sticks for a fire in the fireplace thoughtfully provided in the dining-room of the lodge. There was of course no food of any kind, and the two or three men who were now hovering about were disinclined to help. As for the knowledgeability of the ranger staff, the experience that followed removed all my misgivings.

When at last a ranger showed up, it was his advice that if I intended to roam the Park that night, we had better drive to Kisli, at the Park entrance, where a senior ranger who was said to know all there was to know, particularly of tiger, was resident. So off we went. We had not been on the hill road for five minutes before a loping hyena ran out in front of the car, and stupidly continued to do so for several hundred yards without stepping out to the side. My ranger watched the hyena for a few moments and suddenly ejaculated, 'Tiger! tiger!' I thought here was a fellow with a sense of humour—even if an unusual one. No, he was absolutely serious. Seeing there was no visible reaction from me, he prodded me and called again, 'Tiger! tiger!' I was nonplussed, and thought perhaps he said it to please the visitor, who, for all he knew, might not know the difference between a goat and a sheep—or a hyena and a tiger. I rebuked him, and he quickly corrected himself. Of course, he said, it was a panther, not a tiger. I gave him a dirty look, said nothing, and drove on.

A few minutes later, the whole performance was repeated! Another and larger hyena appeared in our front and did exactly as the other—ran for several hundred yards along the curving and twisting road before stepping out of the way. As soon as he appeared, the ranger shouted again, 'Tiger! tiger!' What he then needed to be told, he was told.

At Kisli, the old forest ranger displaced the young one as my guide and mentor. He announced that the place was crawling with tigers, and only a short while before tigers had been calling to the left and to the right, from north, south, east, and west. He had not the slightest doubt that if we drove around the forest paths, he would show me not only a few tigers, but also some leopards. I said that one tiger would be just grand. Asked how many tigers there were in the Kisli area of the Park, he replied there must be at least thirty! I began to have grave doubts about his reliability. Perhaps the staff were all well trained to

please visitors, particularly on the subject of tigers, but this
visitor was certainly the wrong type on whom to try on these
blandishments. Far from being pleased at this abundance of
tigers, I had begun to feel exactly the opposite.

I knew the old man was going to do just one thing that night,
and that was to take me for a ride. I went, nevertheless. For the
next three hours we drove, circled, doubled on our tracks, and
even got out of the car and looked into the utter black. We dived
into *nullahs* and out of them, making infernal noises which would
have frightened all thirty tigers away. Would not the noise
drive away the tigers? No, my guide assured me, not at all.
They were not shy in his Park. As the night advanced, and with
it the cold, the ranger became less and less voluble, and broke
what was now a very dignified silence less and less often. But
when at last I began to show signs of impatience and suggested
we return, he to Kisli and I to Kanha, he reassured me that
we could not fail to see tiger, a tiger—I marked the present
singular after the earlier plurals—*if* we drove around long
enough. Ah! that was the snag. He could always say we had not
been out *long* enough or tried *hard* enough! I continued to make
impatient noises. But, wait, he confided, only the day before a
tiger had been seen lying on the verandah of Kisli resthouse, and
was sure to be *somewhere* around. I turned the car to Kisli, left
him at his hut, and beat it to Kanha, to crawl into a freezing
bed—perhaps the very one in which the friend of my host in
Jabalpur had had his remarkable experience some years
previously.

My friend had made an excursion to Kanha with his companion and, arriving late, had retired to bed, with an arrangement with the *khansama*, or cook-bearer, of the lodge that they
should be awakened at four o'clock in the morning, when they
proposed to go into the Park to see wild life at dawn. What
transpired that night became, subsequently, a funny story.

The friend's friend heard noises at the door of his room, and
assuming it was the *khansama* bringing in the early morning tea,
got out of bed and opened the door. There, not two feet in front
of him, was standing a tiger. Too frightened to shut the door or
to yell, he dived back into the bed, throwing all the bedclothes
over him, and lay shivering with fright. The tiger, apparently as
surprised as the man, bolted. When the *khansama* arrived in due

course with the tea, he was alarmed to see the wide-open door. Entering the room, he saw there was only a heap of clothes on the bed, and concluded the visitor had been carried away by a tiger. With a yell, he rushed to the door of the room where my friend was sleeping and, pounding it, shouted the story of the night's tragedy. My friend rushed to the other room where it did not take him long to find that the bed, far from being unoccupied, had an occupant who clung to it tenaciously in spite of the vigorous shaking administered to him and who, from within the bedclothes, was screaming that the tiger had returned and was carrying him away. Time sorted everything out and soothed the nerves of the man who went to Kanha to see tigers, but not at two-feet distance.

L

VII

TWO GREAT WILD OXEN

... for the book of nature has no beginning, as it has no end.
Open the book where you will, and at any point of your life,
and if you have the desire to acquire knowledge you will find it
of intense interest, and no matter how long or how intently
you study the pages, your interest will not flag, for in nature
there is no finality.

JIM CORBETT

INDIA'S TWO GREAT WILD OXEN, the gaur (*Bos gaurus*), or so-
called Indian bison, and the wild buffalo (*Bubalus bubalis*), are
also the largest wild oxen in the world. A good adult bull of
either animal may weigh a ton and stand well over six feet at
the shoulder. Opinions differ as to which is larger; the buffalo
lacks the gaur's dorsal ridge and may not be quite so tall at the
shoulder, but with the great sweep of its horns appears the more
formidable animal. Both are magnificent-looking, and adult
bulls are unafraid of any other animal of the jungles they inhabit. Tigers attack unaccompanied young, and sometimes the
cows, but, unless two are hunting together, generally leave the
grown bulls well alone.

The name of bison as applied to the gaur is incorrect, but it is
widely known in India by that name. Similarly, in North
America, they refer to their bison, the genuine variety, as the
buffalo.

Gaur had an extensive range and lived in good herds in the
hill forests of the Western Ghats, also extending in a north-
easterly direction to the foothills of the Himalayas and Assam,
and to Burma and Malaya. In Malaya, it is called the seladang
and said to reach large proportions, whether in excess of Indian
animals I do not know. Seladang, particularly, have been
credited with a fierce temper and a revengeful nature by many

hunters; perhaps they have been even more persecuted than in India. Gaur in India, where they are not pursued, are mild-mannered and peaceable beasts. This may not be what a certain type of reader of hunting accounts wants, but it corresponds closely to facts. I remember some years ago reading an article on a gaur-hunting trip in India by an American sportsman, in what is perhaps the best-known American sporting magazine, which started with the electrifying statement, 'Every bison is a killer'. The article was decorated with drawings of snorting and charging gaur, with the intrepid hunter in a variety of perilous positions, hanging from the low branch of a tree, or clearing a very wide *nullah* in one splendid leap. Both the story that was told and the illustrations were clearly the products of a vivid imagination. Injured severely, or persistently annoyed, the gaur can be expected to give a very good account of itself, but to vest it with a fierce and aggressive temper is more fanciful than truthful.

Much of the gaur's shooting from the last century has oc-curred in the lower Western Ghats, where the finest herds have lived. But, as already stated, this tract of country has suffered greatly from all manners of projects, wholly unco-ordinated from the angles of conserving the forests and the land and protecting the wild life and its migratory routes. The loss of forests on a big scale, combined with heavy shooting, has exterminated the gaur from many parts of its range in hill and plateau country. It survives primarily in the Periyar, Mudu-malai, and Bandipur Sanctuaries in this part of India, with isolated and small herds or lone bulls scattered about the rest of its habitat in the Western Ghats. In northern India and Assam, small herds are left in many parts, often the sanctuaries only. But everywhere there is the ever-present danger from the poacher.

I have seen gaur in many areas of its habitat, but the best herds have occurred in Periyar and Bandipur. Here Bandipur includes Mudumalai, as the two sanctuaries adjoin, and the animals freely cross from one to the other. My last visit to Bandipur in 1965 included the filming of gaur as one of the main objectives. I was accompanied by the forest ranger Mayappa on my searches for it, and he made an excellent com-panion. We started by driving to a favourable part of the sanctuary, where we left our vehicle. Walking in the forest, we soon saw our first herd of gaur as great, dark blobs under a thick canopy of trees and in an undergrowth of ferns and grass. Progress was difficult, and the great heads looked up as we stepped on and cracked a fallen twig. We froze, they resumed feeding, and we moved forward again. But gaur have good ears, and soon they had had enough of this. They turned and faded away wraith-like into the dark interior, and we ran forward. The light cleared as we reached the steep bank of a *nullah*, and there were the beasts on its far side, still going. They were heading straight for Mudumalai, and the chase had to be given up.

We then came upon another, larger, herd which we followed for the next half-hour in an exciting, stumbling chase over rock, boulder, and bush, and across brushstrewn ravines. A Kuruba lad of perhaps ten years had been watching the herd when we arrived. Kurubas are the aboriginal inhabitants of these hills, and are splendid trackers who were much sought after by sportsmen in the great hunting years of the past. The boy attached himself to us, and as the herd began to move, he motioned us to follow him and, light-footed as a sprite, went off in their pursuit. We were hard put to follow him, the more so as he had a knack of disappearing before our very eyes and reappearing far ahead, while we stopped, really to get our breath back, but pretending it was for the purpose of locating him.

The herd, however, was very much on the alert, and when the animals stopped, it was to throw up their heads, sniff the wind, and flick their tails. If the stop was of some duration, they formed themselves in a wide arc and faced towards us, thus indicating that they were restless and suspicious. Young calves were, however, frisky and suckled their mothers. There was one very young calf, golden-coloured and very beautiful. Had we used a riding elephant, I am sure we could have got closer to this herd, as wild life is very tolerant of elephant, gaur as much as any other animal, and do not seem to take notice of what there is on top of the elephant's back, provided no noises or movements are made and that there are no smells. I did what filming I could of this herd before we decided we could not keep up the pursuit.

That night, after my meal, I decided to go into the forest for a walk before turning in. Presently I was joined by a pariah dog, one of the group which hung about the camp, living off the castaway food from the resthouses and the staff quarters. As I stopped to welcome him, he joyfully responded, and soon made his intentions clear. He was going to stay with me, as, perhaps not without knowledge of the dangers to the like of him from some of the jungle beasts, he needed to be with me if he too was to enjoy the walk and the solitude. Many times we stopped together, and I talked to him, and he came up and looked at me eagerly. He was a gentle, docile beast, who lived a lifetime of hardship and injury, as the tribal children often stoned the camp dogs unmercifully. That evening I had just been in time to stop an urchin from pushing a rock nearly as big as himself on the head of a sleeping dog. I was surprised at the trust of my companion, as it would have been the natural thing for him to have kept away from all humans, from none of whom he received kindness, only hurt. The vast stillness around me, its mystery and its glory, yet unscarred by man, was beauty in itself. But the simple trust of the ill-used beast was a kind of beauty too.

Gaur remained difficult in the days that followed. We followed other herds, and sometimes solitary animals. At last, on the very last evening, the biggest bull of them all made up for the bad manners of his tribe. Big bulls, even when still in their prime, sometimes leave the herd and lead solitary lives. He was no doubt one such. It was semi-dark, and we were standing on a forest path. At first, all that showed were his curved and rugged horns, somewhat worn to bluntness, as he scrambled up from a *nullah* bed. His great black head slowly came into view, and then his magnificent blue-black bulk showed in the wild dusk now all around us. He was truly another monarch of the wilderness, and we watched in silence as, only a few feet away, he swung leisurely along in the low grass, crossed the rugged path along which we had come, and turned away from us to disappear into the trees. It was a moving climax to a trip in which I must have seen fifty head of gaur, but none as close as this mighty beast.

Gaur should do well in the southern Indian sanctuaries, provided protective measures are strengthened. Even many years ago in Periyar, I was told that a dead gaur was worth in the region of Rs.300 to a poacher, who sells the meat in village markets, and also the skin and horns, the latter being carved into a variety of curios, commonly seen in tourist shops in Kerala, Mysore, and Madras. The great mounted heads one so often sees in prime gaur country, with horn-spreads of forty inches, are of course gone now. A thirty-inch spread is a very good one today, but for those of us who have not seen the giants of yesterday the giants of today are quite enough justification to urge their conservation.

Gaur do not, for some reason, thrive in zoo conditions, and I do not think there are many captive specimens. As no post-mortems are carried out after the deaths of captive animals, with the exception of Calcutta's Zoo, the cause of death is only surmised and remains unknown. Gaur are easily infected from domestic cattle, and epidemics among wild herds have been known to decimate the numbers. Inoculation of cattle let out to graze in forest grasslands has been tried in the past with success in restricted areas, Coimbatore in the south and Mandla in Madhya Pradesh for example, but I doubt if it is being widely employed anywhere today.

Gaur have sometimes interbred with domestic cattle but only in Assam and Burma; why not in southern India, no one seems to know. The hybrid, of which I have included a photograph, is sometimes called the mithun, sometimes the gayal. These hybrids apparently live in a semi-wild state in the vicinity of villages, but I do not know if they are put to any use. It seems unlikely. The mithun is massive like the gaur, but has straight, instead of curved, horns.

The wild buffalo was once widely distributed over the grass jungles and riverain forests of the Gangetic plain, the *terai*, Assam, and eastern peninsular India down to the river Goda-vari. Many are the accounts of hunting it which appear in the diaries and books of British sportsmen of the last century and the early part of this century. The buffalo was shot down much more speedily and efficiently than the gaur, no doubt because its habitat was more open, but certainly not because it was a less worthy antagonist, for a wounded or enraged buffalo is a highly dangerous beast. Buffalo have always preferred marshy, grass-grown jungles in the vicinity of rivers and lakes where it is easier to locate them, while gaur retire to hilly and forest tracts where tracking them is much more difficult. Buffalo also enter cultivated fields in search of growing grain, and make good targets to the firearms of the villagers.

The consequence of all this has been that the buffalo has been largely exterminated, and must be considered as needing total and effective protection if it is to survive in the wild state. It survives only in a few sanctuaries in Assam, and a pocket or two in Orissa and Madhya Pradesh. A mere handful may be left in the Kosi river valley in Nepal. J. C. Daniel and B. R. Grubh made a survey in 1965 in peninsular India, and concluded that not more than about 400 animals were left in Orissa and Madhya Pradesh. This, taken together with Gee's 1965 estimates of 1,425 for Assam and 20 for Nepal, puts the total of the Indian wild buffalo at about 1,845 head.

In north Bengal, where they lived in abundance, often in herds of hundreds, and where in parts habitat is still excellent for their living, they have become extinct from incessant shooting. In the *terai* and riverain jungles west of this tract, where lived some of the most magnificent herds in history, it has likewise been eliminated. This includes a famous buffalo habitat in the valley of the Gandak river, where at Bhaisolotan, at the Indo-Nepalese border and a famous beauty spot, a dam is being built as the river debouches from the foothills into the plains. In the great swamp-jungles of the Sunderbans in the southern extremity of Bengal, also one of their historic habitats, buffalo have been extinct for many years.

The two largest concentrations of buffalo today are in the Kaziranga and Manas Sanctuaries, estimated at about 700 and 400 animals out of the Assam total of 1,425. Small herds are left in the Sankosh valley just west of Manas, in the Sonairupa, Orang, and Laokhowa Sanctuaries in central Assam, and in the Pabha, or Milroy, Buffalo Reserve and east Lakhimpur in eastern Assam. The Manas animals are reputed to be the best and carrying the biggest horns. The Kaziranga herds are good too, and can be approached fairly close on elephant-back provided it is done with circumspection—not always possible except with the best *mahouts*. Solitary animals and groups in twos and threes fled quickly, but the herds were less inclined

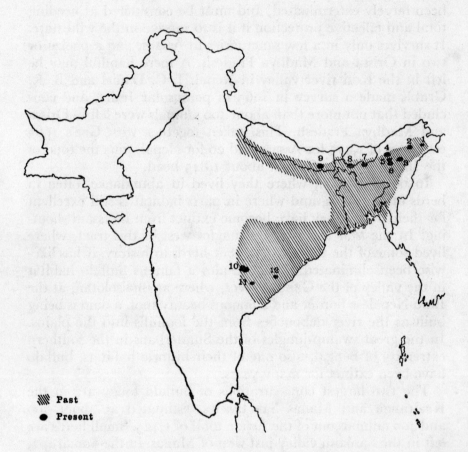

MAP 4
Past and present distribution of the wild buffalo. Survival areas are; 1 East
Lakhimpur; 2 Pabha; 3 Kaziranga; 4 Sonairupa; 5 Orang; 6 Laokhowa;
7 Manas; 8 Sankosh; 9 Kosi (Nepal); 10 Indravati; 11 Talperu; 12
Kondakamberu

39 Himalayan tahr kid, which was caught near Darjeeling and taken to the Himalayan Zoological Park there. However it died after a few days

40 Sambar stag, Mudumalai Sanctuary
41 Sambar hind and young, Mudumalai Sanctuary

42 Chital stag with fine antlers in low bush cover, Mudumalai Sanctuary
43 Party of swamp deer, Kaziranga Sanctuary. Antlers are regenerating

44 Mouse deer in the Mudumalai Sanctuary in summer
45 Mithun bull. A mithun is a cross between a gaur and a domestic cow

46 Lone gaur bull near the Moyar river, Mudumalai Sanctuary
47 Gaur herd in natural teak forest, Mudumalai Sanctuary

48 Buffalo in Kaziranga Sanctuary

49 Sarus crane, Mysore, in winter   50 Openbilled stork, Ranganthittoo

Kaziranga Sanctuary, January   51 Blacknecked stork   52 Lesser adjutant

to panic. Even in a herd, if calves are present, the cows move them farther as one gets closer.

The biggest buffalo were often the solitary ones. Occasionally a big bull may be seen grazing with a smaller bull. Various theories have been advanced to account for the solitary existence of the big bulls, and of these two seem likely: one, that they prefer to live in this way in any case, only rejoining the herd for mating, and the other, that they are dispossessed master bulls which have had their day and been supplanted by a younger and stronger bull. Buffalo bulls known to visit domestic herds and serving cows on the fringes of grass jungles probably belong to the latter category.

In Kaziranga, where large herds of domestic buffalo graze in the sanctuary, mating of wild bulls with domestic cows seems to be common. It is possible, therefore, that not all of Kaziranga's buffalo are wild. Many may be feral—not a desirable state, as ultimately their presence must lead to deterioration of the wild stock.

Where a wild bull decides to serve domestic cows, there is little the herdsman can do, unless he wants to invite the village *shikari* to kill off the visitor. Apparently, however, he does not object to the wild admixture. The offspring are big and strong, but I have been told of cases where cows died in the process of calf-birth, as the calves were too big for normal delivery. The offspring may also be less tractable than wholly domestic calves. But where there are wild buffalo in the neighbourhood, a certain admixture is inevitable and admitted as a doubtful blessing by the herdsmen.

When the wild bull arrives, the domestic bulls are in grave danger, as the newcomer begins his reign by killing off all of them. In such a case, the domestic bulls are caught and castrated and used for ploughing and other tasks, rather than let them run the risk of being killed. Strangely, the wild bull has no interest in gelded domestic bulls.

I was once told of the story of a wild bull which, on joining a domestic herd, promptly killed two of the six bulls of the herd. The other four fled into the jungle and were never seen again. The wild bull stayed with the herd for some six months, and performed the duties of all the tame bulls. By that time, he had become a shadow of his old self. Suddenly, one day he disappeared, and never came back—no doubt realizing he had made a grave mistake.

Wild bulls frequenting forest villages in quest of cows become tame to a surprising degree. From villagers' accounts, it appears that they take no notice of other domestic animals or of children who often accompany the grazing cows. But they promptly resent the presence of adult humans. Another interesting piece of information was that, during the period of his possession of the herd, the large predators, tigers and leopards, leave the herd animals alone. To that extent he seems to safeguard the herd.

In peninsular India surviving buffalo are in considerable danger, as development projects are already under way in their tracts. Examples are the large iron ore project in Bastar, and the Balimela dam project in Orissa which will submerge the Kondakamberu valley, where the last survivors in that State now live. More of their habitat is being demanded for cultivation, such as for use by the Gonds, the aboriginal inhabitants of the tract who, after practising shifting cultivation for so long, are showing signs of settling down to more permanent ways. This in time will further affect the buffalo as, with growing crops, they will follow the cultivated fields and thus leave themselves open to more persecution. The former inaccessibility of their habitat protected the buffalo in this part of India. The tracts are now no longer inaccessible, and danger to the animal has correspondingly increased. There is a proposal for a buffalo sanctuary in Bastar, but if it is not brought into being at once, I am afraid it will not be long before the last buffalo in southern India is exterminated.

I have seen good buffalo heads, but they cannot compare with those of Sir Samuel Baker who wrote of horns of more than ten feet measured from tip to tip across the forehead. A head of eight-and-a-half feet must be considered exceptional today. Baker, incidentally, referred to buffalo in Ceylon in the late nineteenth century. This being so, not all of Ceylon's wild buffalo can be feral, as they are often said to be. I have seen buffalo in Ceylon's Ruhuna National Park, and some were just as good as the Indian buffalo.

Wild buffalo are not much different-looking from domesticated ones, except in their size and the sweep and symmetry of their horns. The horns of domestic buffalo grow to all sorts of shapes and twist and curve unnaturally, with grotesque results. The spread of horn of the wild ones not only exceeds that of the domestic animals, and indeed that of any member of the family *Bovidae*, but are magnificent in their wide sweep and majesty. This is not to say that an occasional wild animal will not have a deformed horn, but while deformation is the rule in a tame buffalo in the East, it is the exception in a wild one.

Apart from man, the wild buffalo has few enemies. Tigers may attack calves and immature animals, but seldom the adult beast. Two tigers may hunt a full-grown bull or cow, though I have not come across an eyewitness account of such an attack, only those recorded by inference after an incident believed to have taken place.

The protection of the buffalo will remain a difficult matter. Its best chances of survival are in the declared sanctuaries, and in the hope that more will be created where it still exists. Outside of them, it seems unlikely to survive. As with gaur, buffalo are prone to cattle diseases, and many cases of decimation of herds have been recorded both in peninsular India and in Assam from epidemics contracted from village cattle grazing in the jungles.

Buffalo survival can be further assisted by its reintroduction into the Jaldapara Sanctuary in north Bengal, as its riverain jungles are ideal for it as a home, and as it indeed lived in plenty in all the riverain tract of this region once. Jaldapara is rich in vegetation and offers good cover for retirement, but its chief handicap is its odd shape which is that of an inverted 'V', north to south. Between the two legs are cultivated fields dotted with tiny villages. Poaching from these vantage points has often been a problem. Rhino steal into the cultivation rarely, but buffalo will no doubt do so more often. Crop protection justifies the killing of wild life in India, but even this is not necessary. Apart from the villagers, such areas within a sanctuary give the poacher a forward base for his nefarious operations. There was a small estate within the Periyar Sanctuary in the far south of India where poachers could make their headquarters on payment of a sum of money to the owner of the estate, the amount depending on the kind and number of animals the poacher intended to kill. No questions were asked, and everyone was happy.

There is a third wild ox, the banteng (*Bos banteng*) or tsaine, with its main range in Burma and south-east Asia, but extending to the hills of Manipur. Whether it still lives within Indian limits is not known. It is a smaller version of the gaur, but massive still, and is distinguished from the gaur by lack of the high dorsal ridge which so suddenly dips and disappears at about half-way on the back in the gaur. Trickles of information from Burma and south-east Asia point to the fact that the banteng has disappeared from many of its former haunts through heavy slaughter by forest tribesmen. Protection is so ineffective as to be non-existent in the chaotic conditions of most of that vast region.

VIII

THE TWILIGHT OF
THE ANIMALS

Man has lost his capacity to foresee and to forestall. He will
end by destroying the earth.

ALBERT SCHWEITZER

'THE NATURAL WILDERNESS is a fragile thing; the material of
poetry, art and music.' Thus said the late Dr. Olaus J. Murie,
the distinguished American naturalist. As I now come to the
end of my sad story of the ebbing fortunes of the wild life of
India, my thoughts go back, now to a night spent in the wilderness in the north of this wonderful country, now to a day spent
in the south, slices of time spent in the 'fragility' of the wild
world even such as Dr. Murie spoke of.

I remember that first evening in the Chandraprabha Forest
as I sat in an easy-chair outside the lodge, of which I was the
sole occupant. The setting sun made a scene of splendour, as its
rays struggled with the flying mist-cloud fronting the waterfall
just beyond me. The water's roar seemed merely to accentuate
the stillness around. The great copper-gold sun was poised
deceptively still on the far edge of the forest, while in reality
it was plunging fast beyond the western horizon. The long rays
caught the treetops for a few moments, and all at once the great
orb seemed to disappear with a rush and the forest around me
was draped in a black hush. The trees stood motionless in the
still air as if welded to the landscape and their dark outlines
were silhouetted against the heavens, now beginning to be
star-studded.

There was the morning after, when I was up and off, accompanied by the considerate forest ranger, Sukhraj Singh,
long before dawn. It was fragrant and cool as we drove through
forests beyond the sanctuary in perfectly delightful country,

hills of the extreme eastern end of the Vindhyas, umber and pinkish in the background in the early morning light. The dawn was not abrupt as the dusk had been, and as the blurred outlines of the forest assumed shapes, bird song twittered from the trees. The sun arose and fought off the ground mist, revealing herds of white and brown cattle or big, black buffalo, already on the move for the eternal business of grazing. Sheet-swathed cowherds followed them listlessly and looked at us without interest. Suddenly, like a sprite, a pretty little chinkara buck stepped up to the roadside, and as quickly vanished into the parklike interior of the forest.

Later that day, as we were returning to the lodge after a long and tiring trek into the sanctuary's interior, I remember the little village in our way, perfectly harmonious with the wilderness around it, from which little cascades of grey-white smoke drifted into the sky. The smell of these fire-plumes mingled with the evening smells of the forest, as the toothless old man we asked for news of lion looked uncomprehendingly at us. Bird calls and the pad-crunch of our feet were the only noises in the stillness. We walked on, stopping only to look at a sloth bear's pawprints as it had shuffled from a cattle path into thick bush.

There was the memorable night in the great forests of the Godavari river, when with the forest officer of the range I spent fourteen hours cruising in our jeep with scarcely a stop. He had told me that development projects had destroyed most of the wild life, but I hoped to see the wild things once the night had spread its protective and kindly shroud over the glorious wine-colour of the evening teak forests. The tall trees blushed like copper in the setting sun as we set out from the forest lodge. Soon would be the hour when the peacocks would step out of their roosts, the males to play their dazzling court to the downright hens—the enchanted hour of the Indian jungle. It was a crisp evening, typical of the cold weather.

We were armed with the fell combination of jeep and spot-light, but our purpose was not to kill. I wanted to see how the animals that were left in these once-pristine forests lived in the changed circumstances. The first hour and the next passed without the forest showing anything but the peacocks, but I was not unduly despondent. Teak forests have very little undergrowth, and we had clear vision as we drove in and out of them. The first major encounter was as unexpected as it was magnificent. Across an irrigation canal, now dry, we caught in our roving lights a group of three chital stags, an uncommon party, two already so disturbed as to be hurrying down the far side of the embankment. But the third and the most splendid of the three, with his great antlers in velvet, stood still for a few seconds in the light-beam now trained solely on him, nostrils quivering, and made an unforgettable sight.

Every now and then we stopped to savour the stillness and to draw into ourselves the warm, gentle breeze which blew through the pillared trees all around us. Sometimes a bird sang like a tinkling bell as it flew home, rather late, to roost. Now we heard the sound of running water, tossing and swirling, in a jungle stream, although most *nullahs* were semi-dry at this time of year. As we passed a project area, now here, now there, we heard the babel of cutting, sawing, or hammering in the palpitating air. We hastily fled from the offending noises, away into the dark stillness, weaving in and out of the teak trees, picking out dead tree stumps and ravines in the headlights and avoiding them when we could, or crashing through when we could not.

We began to pick up numerous pairs of eyes in the light beam, but identification was difficult. Since I was going to be the one to make the novel attempt to take the photographs of their owners by flashlight, as my companion held the animal with his lights, by walking deviously and circuitously in the surrounding darkness to get as close to the quarry as possible, I did not like to base my effort on a rapid identification and walk on to a resting sloth bear or an irate leopard. The fallen leaves were dry and crackled noisily as I stepped on them in the utter blackness. Many times, as I got close to a nilgai or a sambar, the animal started to move off but still in the light, and I followed it for as long as I could simply for the pleasure of it.

There was a sloth bear, a round black bundle of fur, who melted away as the beam strayed to him. There were sambar and nilgai in ones and twos, almost always near the fringes of forest villages and inside fenced-in teak nurseries. I wondered what it was in the latter that attracted them. The numerous thatch-roofed platforms on bamboo poles in the cornfields were mute evidence of the incursions of deer, antelope, and pig, in search of the sweet, growing corn. Fleeing nilgai were comic with their little tails stuck straight up in the air. A pair of porcupines, husband and wife we presumed, moved as if they were on wheels, a continuous progression forward, feet never showing, only a flurry of quills. We drove parallel with them for a while, before they gave us the slip by a quick right turn into thorny bush, strictly penetrable only by porcupines. We saw more of them, but only singly or in pairs. It was the same uninterrupted movement, terribly purposeful in its forward slide-march, as if the animals had a date with destiny.

We put on an extra layer of clothing as the wind blew colder. Of jungle noises there were none, and no wonder. The ruthless slaughter of the preceding years had made all animals both wary and shy. We drove up a hill through a long, winding, and beautiful forest path, and it grew even colder. By the pathside stood a magnificent nilgai bull, feeding. Momentarily dazzled by the light, he stood still for perhaps five seconds. What an easy target these animals make, I thought, for the jeep-and-spotlight hunter! Recovering himself, he turned and ran into the forest.

The magic wand of dawn was already touching the tattered leaves of the great trees as we started on the long and weary drive back. The beauty was as transient as the wild animals we had seen. On this trip we had spent fourteen continuous hours in these jungles, and as we stepped out of the jeep another day had established itself.

Then there was our family week in the Hazaribagh National Park, of the kind we often talked about in our pedestrian and contentious city life. The two boys, very young then, had already begun to be imbued with our longing for nature's prodigalities and to share them with us. Our longing to get away from the worship of time and the banal details of appointments and teas had finally worked itself into a pattern—thrice a year in the wilderness, taking my annual leave in three parts to coincide with the school holidays of my wife, who was teaching, and of the boys who were in a public school. We were asked if it was safe to camp with small children amongst wild animals. Our secret lay in the fact that the boys thought of these animals as their particular *friends*. Animals, as a rule, prefer to bite the faint-hearted. They know if you are calm, if you are friendly, or if you are scared. A leopard may be unsociable, but he may be reckoned upon to leave you alone. A bear may be inquisitive, but has no reason to attack you unless you surprise him.

The forests were not village-free. People lived in their midst in tiny communities of mud-built and tumbledown huts, with pungent, musty, rotting smells. We spoke to village folk with betel-stained smiles, and watched the unrehearsed grace of their movements and the unchaperoned conversation of men and women, boys and girls. Our boys were continually in a high state of joyful excitement, and spoke of the numerous accidental meetings they hoped to have with animals of the forest. They came with us on foot into the heavily foliaged jungle, where the fecundity of the undergrowth was prodigious, and we stuck to the tracks smoothed by generations of animal feet. There were big tracts where no grass-grown ruins or green-grown moats, not uncommon in India's forests and suggesting man's intrusion in the long past, marred the landscape.

We listened with new ears to the whisper of the trees as they rippled in the cool north wind, and were enfranchised by bird song. If we were out early in the morning, we would get our feet very wet with the night's dew, but it was cool and soothing. We could see the sun drawing up the moisture in spirals of vapour. This was the time of day too when, as they dried, unknown herbs gave off their rich and cloying smells, and the children delighted in plucking and crushing leaves to savour the subtly different and spicy smells. Every sparkling stream in the woods carried an invitation to plunge naked into it. Often it was so marvellously still that their splurges of fun were the only sounds that sweetened the air. The pleasantly warm winter sun turned our skins from their forlorn seedy city look to a healthy brown. In the afternoons, between visits to the Park interior, as we lay on the grass and the sun threw its golden girdles round the canopies of trees, it was warmly sensuous enough to make us feel slumbrous, and yet not go off to sleep. We saw the boys with half-closed eyes, trapped in the city to live human lives, here chasing in and out of the wavering shadows, and heard their yelps of delight as they discovered a brilliantly coloured beetle or butterfly or the gossamer-spun home of a spider, or fed a cheeky little squirrel or wild bird

M

which returned their friendliness by accepting a crumb from their outstretched hands. We lingered, listened, and watched the overflow from the reservoir next to the lodge, over the stone dam, which became an iridescent and glittering waterfall, and the water leaping and gurgling at its foot. The civilized world seemed far away, but the days fled, and we measured them not by their length but by their breadth. It was not all joy; sometimes a strange melancholy would flow over us, but even this had a mellow, unobtrusive beauty of its own. When the time came to leave, it was significant that even the children had nothing to say.

A remarkable fact in the world's history of the last two thousand years is that mankind has disputed all along the line the claims of wild animals to survive in their own right. If their survival was of no use to him—or so he thought—they had to go. The process of extermination of many species of animals has proceeded steadily during the Christian era, but was greatly accelerated after 1800. Today, over a thousand species and subspecies, at a conservative estimate, are treated as gravely threatened. With the apathy to wild life conservation and man's insatiable greed, the fact must be faced that many of these endangered animals will be extinguished in the next two or three decades at the rate of well over a species per year.

Till man appeared on the scene, an uneven increase of any one species was kept down by many natural causes: scarcity of food, predatory animals, disease, natural calamities. That is, a balance was maintained between the reproductive capacity of the species and the natural agencies of destruction—the so-called balance of nature. When man emerged from his savage state, he upset the balance. Animals whose flesh he coveted were killed off, while others he favoured multiplied. Thus, while some animals went over the edge once and for all, others spread and became pests.

It was only at the beginning of this century that thinking men began to appreciate that the wild things too had a right to live, within their habitats, side by side with man. Out of this thinking grew attempts to afford some measure of protection to wild life by the formulation of restrictive laws against indiscriminate shooting. In time, wild life areas here and there were closed in full or in part to shooting, and trapping of animals and trade in pelts and feathers were brought under some kind of control where such was possible. But the magnitude of the problem was so vast, and the general indifference of governments and the public so great, that these measures were woefully inadequate and touched only the fringe of the problem. The spiritual and cultural values of wild life conservation remained largely unappreciated, and the scientific interest in the fauna did not extend beyond the naturalists.

This, then, is the position today in all parts of the world, to a greater or to a lesser degree. To appreciate the great wealth of animal life that has already been destroyed, we may take a look at one or two historic destructions. Africa was perhaps the world's greatest reservoir of wild life, but, after the advent of the Boers in South Africa, suffered cruelly. The stupendous antelope and zebra herds were destroyed without trace in an amazingly short number of years. Figures of these killings are hardly credible, and hundreds of thousands of these beasts were slaughtered during the Boer treks inland, comparable in scale only with the bison slaying in North America in the second half of the last century. With increased European occupation in the further north of Africa, professional hunters for ivory and other animal products took up the chase and decimated the equally vast animal congregations of those regions. All this was followed in time by legalized slaughter by white hunters hired to clear the bush on behalf of governments for African settlements or tse-tse fly control, and illegal slaughter by the Africans themselves as political, social, and environmental conditions began to change with a bewildering rapidity.

The curtain rose for wild life slaughter in Asia a long time after the main herds in Africa and North America had been destroyed. In the colonial era, when most of southern Asia was governed either by European nations or by local kings and chieftains, wild animals, although extensively hunted both by Europeans and the local princes and their retainers, were comparatively unaffected in the absence of organized mass-killing, which was the characteristic feature of antelope, zebra, and bison hunts. It was fortunate that this was so, because wild life in Asia did not exist, except in a very few tracts, on the vast African scale. Asia's animals could not have survived man's slaughter on the African style. Their habitats, too, aided their survival, as more often than not the habitats were thick and heavy jungle as against the open plains of Africa and North America.

Since the last war, as the great colonial regimes came to a close, a period of unrest and strife began in many areas, which scattered large-scale destruction of every sort in Burma, Malaya, the new countries of Indo-China, and Indonesia, and is still doing so. India has been notably stable, but while war and law-lessness led to uncontrolled killing of wild animal life in other parts of southern Asia, the immense development projects of India led to habitat-destruction without parallel in history. Today, only a very small fraction of the wild life of twenty-five years ago is left.

Has India's wild life a future? One cannot truthfully say it has, and the reasons have been discussed. One might ask, do these wild animals have to live on? Man in India wants more and more space, the population is increasing at an unprece-dented rate, and has he not the right to clear and occupy the forests as he pleases, killing off the wild life in the process? He certainly has no such right, no claim in the least to apportion to himself all the living-space of so many creatures allotted to them from immemorial time in the natural order of things. What is his right, the right of might and the gun? If progressive thought believes that might without justice is not right, how can such a theory be applied in justification of the slaughter of the animals? Wild life asks for so little of man. It is this which has hit me with the force of a sledge-hammer each time I have set foot in a jungle and seen its wild residents. They ask for nothing except to be left alone in the pathetic strips of wild tract that are all that remain of their once populous homes. The animals have their simple rights too on this earth—to exist. In India, much too often there is pious talk of wild animals being in the cultural traditions of the land, as if this in itself will assure their eventual survival. On the other hand, it merely draws attention away from the problem of saving them.

All I have said about the animals applies equally well to the country's rich avian and reptilian life. Bird life is superbly rich. Including migrants, over 1,500 species find homes in the sub-continent. But they need trees and bushes, water and marshes, and protection from hunters to survive. Today, the most affected are those limited to specific breeding and feeding grounds through deprivation of their territory.

The beautiful pinkheaded duck (*Rhodonessa caryophyllacea*) has been feared extinct for some years. The last authentic record was in Darbhanga district in Bihar in June 1935, a long time ago. The whitewinged wood duck (*Cairina scutulata*) of Assam is so rare as to be nearly extinct. Others like the great Indian bustard (*Choriotis nigriceps*) and the monal pheasant (*Lophophorus impejanus*) are the ornithologists' worry, as they totter on the brink of extinction.

I include a few bird pictures in the book to show that I am not partial to the conservation of mammals only. I have done little photography of birds, and most of the pictures are by Krishnan, the supreme artist in Indian wild life photography.

What is an Indian jungle without its quota of peacocks (*Pavo cristatus*)? Who can forget, once he has seen it, the display of the cock bird before his small harem of hens, in the bewitching hour before dusk? And what a display it is! The erection of the gorgeous ocellated tail, the strutting, the posturing, the paroxysms of quivering! And when it is all over, the harsh '*may-awe*' and the gasping '*ka-aan*'!

What is a marsh landscape without a pair of sarus cranes (*Grus antigone*), the largest birds of India? F. W. Champion called them 'the Darby and Joan of the jungle'. These huge, grey birds, with their long, bright red legs and heads which look as if they were covered with close-fitting caps of ruby velvet ornamented with tassels, are devoted companions—so devoted are they thought to be that tribal hunters who kill one for food kill the other too.

Many must have heard but not seen the collared scops owl (*Otus bakkamoena*), pretty little 'horned' owlet, heard its soft, questioning *wût*? and its lovely ascending note of bubbling pleasure, from out of the groves it is partial to. Some at least must have seen the crested serpent eagle (*Spilornis cheela*) as it has soared in wide circles high up in the sky in wooded country; seen too, perhaps, the openbilled stork (*Anastomus oscitans*) with the gap between his arching mandibles, and the smaller egret (*Egretta intermedia*) in his breeding plumage, in their favourite marshes and mudflats, busily searching for frogs, crabs, and snails.

But one and all must have seen the whitebacked vulture (*Gyps bengalensis*), unloved bird, carrion feeder, useful scavenger, and drawing attention to itself by its quarrels with its mates, hissing and screeching, over an animal carcass in the countryside; seen too, if they had the stomach to wait and watch, the speed with which the flock demolish such remains.

Both kinds of crocodiles of India, the mugger (*Crocodilus palustris*) and the gharial (*Gavialis gangeticus*) have become extremely rare. Both are now officially protected—which does not prevent week-end sportsmen from Calcutta from hunting them in the Sunderbans swamps, where alone the mugger perhaps survives in any number. Both the snub-nosed mugger and the long-snouted gharial were such interesting and integral parts of the Indian jungle scene, and though the mugger is by no means a likeable thing, their passing would sadly deplete the stage.

Another disappearing reptile is the monitor lizard. The last one I saw was crossing the road as I was driving through the Mahanadi Sanctuary in north Bengal in 1964. There is a famous story attached to this lizard. Its best-known characteristic is its very powerful hold when it clings to anything. Tradition has it that when Shivaji, the Great Mahratta, laid siege to the Moghul-held fortress of Khelna, its walls were so steep that all the attempts of his soldiers to scale them were foiled. Then one of two brothers tied a rope to a monitor and threw it to run up the wall. As it found a vantage-point and settled itself, the other brother scaled the wall with the rope's aid, and opened the gates to let in the Mahrattas. Shivaji was so pleased with the achievement that he awarded the title of 'Ghorpade' to the clan from which the brothers came, from the Marathi name for the monitor, which is *ghorpad*. But true it is that it is immensely difficult to dislodge a monitor once it has decided to cling and stay put.

Devoted individuals, and the two premier natural history societies, the Bombay Natural History Society and the Wild Life Preservation Society of India, have worked assiduously for the cause of wild life conservation, and to persuade the authorities to evolve a policy by which the objects of such conservation can be achieved through sustained implementation of its component stages. But for such efforts, the situation today would be far worse. But in a problem of this nature it is increasingly difficult for single persons or non-official groups to act effectively.

No one can now dispute that the wild life of a country is not one of its most interesting and valuable assets. Sanctuaries where they have been created in India are for the ostensible purpose of conserving the natural fauna and flora in specific and characteristic areas. I say 'ostensible' because there is so little 'following-up' done to ensure they are adequately staffed and managed. There are no experienced naturalists or former hunters of big game on their staffs to advise Forest Departments on wild life management. Often the men whose supposed task is to look after the wild life in their restricted areas have very little useful knowledge of their charges.

Conservation of wild life should no longer be thought of, as I am sure it is in many high circles, as a frill, an amenity that ranks low in any realistic scale of values. There are economic arguments for it, in addition to the scientific, the aesthetic, and the moral.

It was once the case that wilderness and wild life did not need human aid to survive. Both would indeed have conserved themselves had they been left alone. This, however, has not been the case. Both have been rendered unstable through man's interference, and therefore now need his aid to continue to exist. The science of ecology has thus assumed great importance in recent years. It is the branch of biology which deals with the habits of organisms, their modes of life, and their relations to their surroundings. Wild life no longer exists in merely physical or climatic environments, but in increasingly complex conditions which involve extended relationships with man.

But the utmost care is necessary in all stages of ecological research as applying to the wild life of India, lest conclusions are hastily drawn and universally applied. For example, I read recently a statement by a scientist working on prey-predator balances that these need to be improved in the sanctuaries. I did not understand it at all. In none of the Indian sanctuaries do predators cause any anxiety either because of their numbers or because of their taking too many prey animals. They are all comparatively slow-breeding, and a spectacular increase in their numbers can be quite ruled out. Neither are the prey animals excessive, and under the present conditions they are unlikely to multiply hugely in the foreseeable future. Denudation of forest grasslands is caused by domestic livestock, not by the wild herbivores. I should have thought that no interference whatever was necessary in the prey-predator relationship, as the sanctuaries are populated by too few of either group, not by too many.

In the end, wild life in India will be conserved only if it is kept on a national footing without reference to politics or political units. Time is not on the side of the animals. Conservation of wild life should continue to aim primarily at the maintenance of its habitats. All forest, scrub, marsh, and swamp are in charge of government departments, and the saving of adequate areas of these to provide living-space for the animals is the responsibility of the State.

IX
WILD LIFE SANCTUARIES
OF INDIA

With a heart of furious fancies,
Whereof I am commander;
With a burning spear,
And a horse of air,
To the wilderness I wander.

ANONYMOUS

I GIVE IN THIS CHAPTER a list of wild life sanctuaries in India, picked for their importance in the conservation of wild life generally or of individual species in particular, or for their interest as sanctuaries accessible to tourists and therefore of economic value, or for their potential in the future years. All the major ones are included, and a number of the smaller ones, but none without interest.

In their description, there are difficulties in terminology. The application of the definitions adopted by the Indian Board for Wild Life for the four kinds of areas it recognizes as wild life-conserved areas, to locations in the various States where wild life receives protection of one degree or another by the respective States, varies widely. Consequently, the description of a conserved area as 'national park,' or 'wild life sanctuary,' or 'protected area,' or 'reserve' is not in itself conclusive of its status. Throughout the book I have used 'wild life sanctuary' or 'sanctuary' to mean one or other of these places, as my main purpose was to discuss the present status of the different animals, and only to a very much lesser degree the quality of safeguard vouchsafed to them in particular demarcated areas. I found it to be the only way of doing so, and in order not to create a great deal of confusion in the reader's mind.

The Indian Board for Wild Life has defined the four areas where wild life receives some kind of protection thus:

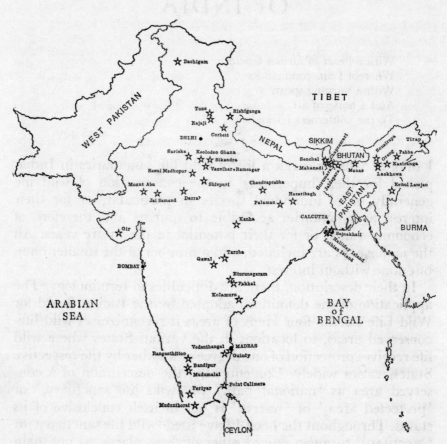

MAP 5
India's wild life sanctuaries

1. A *National Park is*

An area dedicated by statute for all time, to conserve the scenery and natural and historical objects, to conserve wild life therein and to provide for the enjoyment of the same in such manner and by such means as will leave them un-impaired for the enjoyment of future generations, with such modifications as local conditions may demand.

Gee amplified this when he wrote:

In most countries of the world, a National Park can only be created by the national, central or federal government of the country. But under the Constitution of India, 'wild life' is a State Subject and not a Concurrent or Central Subject, and therefore a State Government can constitute a national park in its State Legislature—preferably subject to certain standards which are now being drawn up by the Indian Board for Wild Life.

At the moment some States have created national parks, and some have not. Therefore a wild life sanctuary of one State need not necessarily be inferior to a national park of another State.

2. A *Wild Life Sanctuary* is

An area constituted by competent authority in which killing, hunting, shooting, or capturing of any species of bird or mammal is prohibited except by or under the control of the highest authority in the department responsible for the management of the sanctuary.

Gee again amplified this:

In India a sanctuary is usually created by an Order or Gazette Notification of the State Government.

The weakness of a sanctuary in India is that it can be 'desanctuarized' merely by another Order or Gazette Notification of a State Government, as it is not safeguarded by any proper legislation.

3. A *Protected Area.* The Indian Board for Wild Life describe a Protected Area thus:

In many States there may be areas where it may be considered expedient: (i) to afford special protection to wild life, in order to enable species of wild life which are on the verge of extinction to re-establish themselves, (ii) to afford protection to wild life attracted to water impounded in river valley projects and to other irrigation works; (iii) to afford protection to wild life in and around large towns and sacred places.

Such areas may be constituted by an Order of the Government which may also lay down the degree of protection.

Gee explained:

It should be noted that the protection of wild life does not necessarily imply the protection of vermin. Those wild animals and birds, etc. which are injurious to other animals, or to the long-term interests of man, can be kept under control, or even destroyed altogether in extreme cases, in certain places.

4. A *Reserve* is:

(Reserved) forest, or an area in which wild life is protected, by being so constituted under the Indian Forest Act or other forest law.

All this appears very confusing, and therefore, in my list and descriptions of the sanctuaries, I have been content to indicate the national parks only as such, and refrained from further distinctions. As uniformity in the nomenclature is so lacking, the style by which one of these areas is described is not of great import. What is of great import, however, is the protection afforded to the wild life within the areas set aside.

One other description is often too freely used when referring to these places, quite erroneously, and that is 'game sanctuary'. ('Game' is also used when 'wild life' is meant.) But, clearly, 'game' refers to mammals or birds which are hunted or shot for meat or for sport. In pre-independence India, the use of 'game sanctuary' was perhaps permissible, as most of the sanctuaries then were areas where Princely or Provincial governments attempted to keep the numbers of game animals and birds at a safe level, to prevent their disappearance from shooting or other causes, primarily for the benefit of sportsmen.

The Indian Board for Wild Life has drawn a clear distinction between 'wild life' and 'game'—the former applies where conservation of wild life is concerned, and the latter where sport or the enactment of shooting legislation is the subject.

To the visitor, from abroad and from within the country, there are still wonderful scenes to be seen in the sanctuaries. But wild life is nowhere in such numbers as in Africa's national parks and reserves, so that more patience, and sometimes greater effort, is needed to see them. Many animals have become nocturnal in the face of persecution. Most sanctuaries are visitable only in certain months of the year, the very hot months and the rainy season both having to be ruled out.

Methods of getting about in the sanctuaries also vary widely. Where vegetation is thick or ground conditions are swampy, elephant-back rides are the norm. These of course have the quality of novelty to most people, and are hugely enjoyed. There are places where excursions can only be made in motor-launches; and others in paddle-boats. In the larger sanctuaries, there are motorable roads, and these trips are of course the easiest to make, although they tend to be prosaic in the wild surroundings. But almost everywhere, with inclination, one can get about by foot, though this is not to be recommended except to the hardy and those with some knowledge of the jungle. The best times to see wild life in India are the very early hours of the morning or the late hours of the afternoon. It is then that the animals are on the move for food and water.

When I finished compiling my list of sanctuaries, I suddenly decided to add up their areas and work out the average for one. The total spread came to less than 4,700 square miles—leaving out the Tirap Frontier Tract National Park which is largely unexplored—between forty-seven sanctuaries, making for an average of 100 square miles per sanctuary. This makes a square of forest area of approximately ten miles by ten miles.

It has been accepted even by the Indian Board for Wild Life that management of sanctuaries need not necessarily involve suspension or restriction of normal forest operations, because it is said that the timber and other resources have to be made use of to meet the increasing needs of the people. By this it is suggested that the sanctuaries are not expected to provide total protection to the habitat, only to the fauna. Can it be really true that in a country with a land spread of 1·8 million square miles, of which one-third is required to be under forest, some fifty areas each measuring no more than ten miles by ten miles and distributed fairly evenly over the country, cannot be left alone free of exploitation? It is incredible that it should be claimed that the economy of the nation cannot do without the timber and other resources of these tiny enclaves. It is a question of equating the importance of the sanctuaries and all they represent against the slight extra effort and expense that it may entail to extract the equivalent of their produce from other areas, and transport them to the places of use. The sanctuaries, first of all, have been created because they are unique areas, worth saving for their own sakes. Then why not draw a line at exploitation by leaving them alone? Continued exploitation can only end by leaving them as denuded, or at least severely depleted, spaces, thus destroying the very purpose of their existence. If the Forest Department can cut down the trees in one part of a sanctuary—almost always without adequate super-vision—why cannot trees be cut in another part to meet another need, and who is to tell if the villagers are only picking dead wood or that they are not converting live wood into dead? I have given enough examples of choice areas being converted into bleak and dead country. The same fate lies in store for the sanctuaries, indeed it is overtaking some of them now, in the name of limited exploitation.

If tree-cutting is destructive, overgrazing in sanctuaries by domestic livestock is no less so. This is a terrible problem in India, whose numbers of useless cattle are too widely known the world over to need emphasis. The Hindu attitude to cattle is a tremendous obstacle to any sustained action. Hundreds of thousands of these animals are ruining grasslands everywhere, but little cognizance is taken of this devastation, or, if it is, the problem is dismissed as incapable of solution, since any attempt to check it will be bitterly resisted by the villagers who are the largest owners of the stock, and apparently consider all grassland as free to provide for their animals. But in perpetuat-ing their useless animals they are destroying one of the primary sources of the nation's wealth—its land. In the process, they are depriving another source of wealth—the wild life—of its legitimate food, and passing on the diseases of their sick and starving beasts to healthy wild animals which, lacking immunity to the morbidities of domesticated animals, fall like ninepins in any single epidemic that sweeps their ranks.

Last, but by no means least, poaching needs to be ruthlessly eradicated in the sanctuaries in particular, and generally in other areas outside of them where wild life still exists. It may be that, in the latter areas, a distinction will have to be made, for a time at least, between the villager who kills for meat and the *shikari* and the unlicensed sportsman who kill for profit or for fun. All this is not easy, admittedly. But beginnings in many directions can be made. Officers in charge of wild life protection can be given adequate legal authority to enforce the shooting laws. They can be educated and supported in the application of these laws. The people living in the neighbourhood of sanctuaries can be told why and how these laws are being enforced. Propaganda can be directed so that it reaches the casual sportsmen, to tell them what a useless business their kind of hunting is. Project staff can be restrained from going after animals, and measures written into the administration of projects to see that men employed in it do not take to casual sport. Surely all this is part of the law-enforcement of the land, and if implemented with vigour and determination, the people must come to see it as such.

I do not condemn all shooting, although it is not my nature to undertake it. Where the state of the wild life allows it, licensed shooting can be legitimate sport. Genuine sportsmen have made signal contributions to wild life conservation—by reporting illegal incidents, censusing endangered animal species, and in many other ways. My condemnation is of poaching, under whatever guise it shows its ugly head.

The problems of wild life conservation in India are mainly political and administrative, and only in a very much lesser degree ecological. Therefore, conservation is almost entirely in the hands of the politicians and the administrators, and all the naturalists can do is to cajole and to persuade.

1. *Dachigam*

This northernmost of India's wild life sanctuaries was established in 1951, and is of eighty-three square miles. It is important as offering the last refuge to the hangul, or Kashmir stag. It was the old game preserve of the rulers of Kashmir, and scenically is of great beauty. It comprises two levels, called Upper Dachigam and Lower Dachigam, at 12,000 and 6,000 feet respectively. The two levels represent the summer and winter ranges of the hangul. About 200 of this deer are left.

Poaching is widespread, as was shown when the wild pig of the sanctuary was all but exterminated some years ago. But it survived miraculously, and is now believed to have increased to about seventy-five animals. Other animals which use the sanctuary are black bear, brown bear, and musk deer, but these are not permanent residents.

2. *Tons*

Also known as the Govind Ballabh Pant Sanctuary (after a former Chief Minister of Uttar Pradesh, who later was also Union Home Minister), this is another sanctuary in enchanting mountain scenery. The mountain river Tons flows through it before debouching into the plains. The sanctuary was created in 1955, and is of 368 square miles.

The wild life in this region represents the remnants of the rich and varied fauna of Tehri Garhwal, one of the most famous in Indian sporting history. Snow leopard, black bear, brown bear, musk deer, barking deer, bharal, Himalayan tahr, serow, and goral, all occur. Poaching is unchecked, as there is no surveillance.

3. *Rishiganga*

Also called the Nanda Devi Sanctuary, formed in 1939, this is of 250 square miles, and set in stupendous mountain scenery. It includes within it one of the great peaks of the Himalayas, Nanda Devi, 25,640 feet. The Rishiganga river, rising in the glaciers to its east, flows west through the sanctuary in a great gorge.

This is one of the finest areas in the Himalayas for high elevation fauna. Snow leopard, black bear, brown bear, musk deer, bharal, Himalayan tahr, serow, and smaller mammals such as the red hill fox and marmot are all found here. Bird life is rich and varied. Poaching is a menace, and many valleys are said to be cleared of musk deer, bharal, and tahr. Unfortunately, the sanctuary is a 'paper' one, like the Tons, and there is no supervision. A scheme to grow medicinal plants, introduced by the State Forest Department into the heart of the Rishiganga valley, has added to the prevailing uncertainty.

4. *Rajaji*
Another sanctuary named after a political figure (the first Indian Governor-General, C. Rajagopalachariar), its foothill forests were the scene of many a Viceregal shoot. Created in 1948, of 173 square miles, its wild life is still rich in variety, the fauna being the same as in the more famous Corbett National Park farther east. Elephant, tiger, leopard, sloth bear, sambar, chital, and barking deer are the main fauna.

Conveniently accessible from Delhi, the sanctuary, however, has not been developed for visitors. Nomadic tribesmen, called *gujars*, descending from the mountains in winter in search of pasturelands for their livestock, have wreaked havoc in the sanctuary, at the same time enjoying poaching under security conditions. Timely action may yet save both vegetation and fauna.

5. *Corbett*
One of India's most famous sanctuaries, this was constituted in 1935 as the first National Park. It is tucked within a west-to-south bend of the Himalayan river, Ramganga, and extends over 125 square miles. The scenery in the river valley is majestic, but the loveliest and most important part will be submerged on completion of the Kalagarh dam, lower on the river, in 1973.

Best known for its splendid tigers, the Park also has elephant, leopard, black bear, sloth bear, hyena, wild dog, wild pig, sambar, chital, barking deer, and hog deer. Bird life is very rich. Both kinds of crocodile, mugger and gharial, occur in the river, but are rarely seen. Tourist facilities are well developed. The Park is accessible from November to May.

6. *Sikandra*
In the fifty-acre enclosure around the Tomb of the Emperor Akbar in Sikandra, six miles from Agra, the city of the Taj Mahal, are about a hundred blackbuck. This is a good place to see this antelope, as it is not easily seen in the few sanctuaries in which it is found, being an animal of the plains.

N

7. *Sariska*

This scenic sanctuary with rock canyons, of eighty square miles, is the most important of Rajasthan's eight wild life sanctuaries. It was the former shooting preserve of the rulers of Alwar. Fauna include tiger, leopard, wild pig, sambar, chital, nilgai, and chinkara.

Placed on the National Highway between Delhi and Jaipur, it is easily reached. Facilities for visitors exist. But the sanctuary suffers from overgrazing by thousands of domestic livestock, disturbance from villagers, and poaching.

8. *Keolodeo Ghana*

This eleven-square-mile stretch of marsh and open woodland is the most famous bird sanctuary of India. Formerly the preserve of the rulers of Bharatpur, enormous numbers of wildfowl used to be shot there in the winter months in Princely and Viceregal shoots. It is a natural depression, fed by the monsoon rains and water from the local irrigation works.

From July to October, it is a sanctuary for breeding waterfowl, and the prominent birds are the sarus crane, darter, spoonbill, white ibis, painted stork, grey heron, and large, smaller, and little egrets. In winter, many migratory birds—ducks, geese, pelicans, Siberian cranes, and others—arrive here to feed. A small number of wild pig, chital, nilgai, and blackbuck also live in the dry parts, and an occasional sambar and hog deer. Destruction by cattle-grazing and villagers' activities has been steadily denuding forest and pasture. Within motor reach of Delhi and Agra, the popularity of the sanctuary has been increasing, and tourist facilities exist.

9. *Vanvihar-Ramsagar*

Vanvihar, eleven square miles, and Ramsagar, eight square miles, were two of the finest shooting blocks of the rulers of Dholpur. Maharajah Udaibhan Singh was famous in the 1930s for his wonderful affinities with the animals of the forest. In these reserves, he used to feed every species from his hands sitting in his car, visitors by his side and in the back looking on. The animals included tiger; there was one which specially came to eat cheese!

The blocks comprise low wooded hills of the northern extremity of the Vindhya Range, and hold tiger, leopard, wild pig, sambar, chital, nilgai, and chinkara.

10. *Sawai Madhopur*
The former shooting preserve of the rulers of Jaipur, this sanctuary is of sixty square miles of low outcrop hills of the eastern Aravalli Range. Once famous for its tiger-shooting, it has also leopard, sloth bear, wild pig, sambar, chital, nilgai, and chinkara.

11. *Mount Abu*
This sanctuary of forty square miles is on the Abu plateau and is mainly heavy forest. It represents the western limit of the tiger's range in India, but the appearance of a tiger is exceptional now. Leopard, sloth bear, sambar, chital, and chinkara comprise the fauna. Mount Abu is, of course, famous for its exquisite Jain temples.

12. *Jai Samand*
Another former Princely shooting reserve, this time of the rulers of Udaipur, this is of small spread, twenty square miles of wooded area of the Aravalli Range. The fauna, as in Mount Abu, consists of leopard, sloth bear, wild pig, sambar, chital, and chinkara, with an occasional tiger.

13. *Darrah*
Situated half-way on the plateau between the Aravalli and Vindhya Ranges, Darrah belonged to the rulers of Kotah. Of eighty square miles of well-wooded area, the sanctuary contains tiger, leopard, sloth bear, wild pig, sambar, chital, nilgai, and chinkara.

14. *Shivpuri*
Stepping out of Rajasthan, there is the Shivpuri National Park, established in 1956, of sixty-one square miles, once the game preserve of Gwalior's rulers. It was famed for its tiger-shooting. Soon after independence, neglect led to an alarming decline in wild life from poaching. But there was partial recovery after a sanctuary was declared.

N*

Besides tiger, there are leopard, sloth bear, hyena, wild pig, sambar, chital, and nilgai. The Park is placed on the main Agra-Bombay road and is therefore easily accessible, and is also visitable all through the year. Tourist facilities are good.

15. *Chandraprabha*
This is the so-called second home of the Indian lion. A lion and two lionesses introduced here from Gir have increased to some dozen animals. The sanctuary area is only thirty square miles, yet teak plantations have been introduced into it.

One of the few sanctuaries fenced off from the surrounding forest. Other animals are leopard, sloth bear, sambar, chital, and chinkara. There is no tiger.

16. *Palamau*
Crossing into Bihar, the Palamau forests were the locale of much tiger-shooting in the past. Wild life in general was declining fast when this National Park, also called Betla, of ninety-seven square miles, was declared in 1959. There are tigers left, and elephant, gaur, wild pig, sambar, and chital.

The area is liable to severe drought, and one of unprecedented intensity occurred in 1966–67. Poaching is rampant.

17. *Hazaribagh*
Best known of Bihar's sanctuaries, this National Park was created in 1954 and extends over seventy-five square miles of undulating forest. Wild life was once abundant in this tract, and tigers were common. Poaching, over-exploitation of forest, and domestic grazing transformed the scene. There has been partial recovery, but animals are shy.

There are a few tigers, including possibly a white one, leopard, sloth bear, hyena, wild pig, sambar, chital, and barking deer. There were a few gaur and nilgai, but these seem to have gone.

18. *Mahanadi*
Entering West Bengal, this sanctuary of forty-nine square miles is placed in well-covered hills around the valley of the Mahanadi river (not to be confused with the great river of the same name in Orissa). Fauna include elephant, tiger, gaur, sambar, chital, barking deer, and hog deer. The terrain is difficult, and animals are difficult to see.

19. *Senchal*

This is a high-elevation sanctuary of fifteen square miles, difficult to penetrate, and quite undeveloped. Not far from the famous hill resort of Darjeeling, it is said to have black bear, serow, and goral.

20. *Jaldapara*

Constituted in 1941, this thirty-eight-square mile sanctuary is the most important home of the great onehorned rhinoceros after Kaziranga in Assam. It owes its existence to the distinguished naturalist, the late E. O. Shebbeare, who was in the Forest Department of Bengal. It is mostly riverain forest, interspersed with dense tall grass and criss-crossed with watercourses. The Torsa and other mountain rivers pour through it on their way to the plains, frequently changing their courses. The scenery is beautiful, with the majestic snow-ranges of the Himalayas in the background.

Other fauna are elephant, tiger, leopard, gaur, wild pig, sambar, chital, barking deer, and hog deer, with an occasional black bear, sloth bear, and swamp deer. There are good facilities for visitors.

21. *Gorumara*

A pocket sanctuary of 3·3 square miles, Gorumara lies in a tract which formerly abounded in every kind of large wild animal. Surrounded by open forest, plantations, and cultivation, it is said to contain elephant, rhino, tiger, gaur, wild pig, sambar, barking deer, and hog deer. Many of them must be transient. It is unlikely to have any permanent value in view of its size and its environment.

22. *Chapramari*

Another pocket sanctuary of 3·4 square miles, Chapramari is a little to the north of Gorumara. Said to hold the same fauna as the other, it also can have little long-term significance.

23. *Manas*

This is the westernmost of Assam's many sanctuaries, and is a magnificent wild area, with the river Manas carving its way through it to the plains below in a spectacular gorge. Also known as the North Kamrup Sanctuary, it was notified in 1917, and extends over 105 square miles of riverain forest and grasslands. Apart from Kaziranga, it is the only major refuge for the wild buffalo, of which an estimated 400 live here. Manas buffalo are thought to be the largest alive. There are also elephant, rhino, tiger, gaur, sambar, chital, barking deer, and hog deer. Swamp deer used to be plentiful, but is scarce now. Bird life is rich and varied.

The sanctuary is only partly developed for visitors, and inaccessible in the rainy season. Its potential has been greatly increased since the declaration of a 162-square-mile sanctuary to its north in 1967, in Bhutan and contiguous with it, thanks to the unceasing efforts made by Gee over a period of years. The result is a large wilderness area of heavily forested and unpopulated tract, over which the large animals are free to wander.

24. *Sonairupa*
Sonairupa is in the heart of the great forest belt of Assam, and rather difficult to get to. It is of eighty-five square miles, and an important supplement to Kaziranga with its quota of elephant, rhino, gaur, buffalo, sambar, and hog deer.

25. *Orang*
The Orang Reserve is twenty-four square miles of flat grassland, south of Sonairupa and on the north bank of the great Brahmaputra river. It has a few rhino, gaur, and buffalo.

26. *Laokhowa*
Almost opposite Orang, on the south bank of the Brahmaputra is the Laokhowa Reserve. It also is flat, grassy land, twenty-six square miles, and holds some rhino, gaur, buffalo, and hog deer. Forest exploitation and livestock grazing are affecting this reserve.

27. *Kaziranga*
A world-famous sanctuary and to be made a National Park, Kaziranga has long been the chief home of the great Indian rhino. Established in 1926, it consists of 166 square miles of forest grasslands and heavy swamps on the south bank of the

Brahmaputra. There are believed to be 400 rhino and 700 buffalo in it, the biggest concentrations for either animal any-where. In addition, it has elephant, tiger, leopard, gaur, sloth bear, wild pig, sambar, swamp deer, barking deer, and hog deer. Bird life is abundant.

Rhino on its southern fringe are very tame, and can be seen without fail from elephant-back. Visitors are well provided. The sanctuary gets flooded from the river in the monsoon months, and cannot be visited then. Much of the wild life leaves it at this time and seeks refuge in high ground to the south, running great danger from poachers.

28. *Pabha*
Pabha, or Milroy (after a former Conservator of Forests of Assam who was responsible for its creation), Buffalo Reserve is a small area of nineteen square miles set apart to protect the surviving buffalo in its grass jungles. Elephant and rhino may also occur.

29. *Tirap*
Tirap Frontier Tract National Park at the eastern extremity of Assam, on the Burmese frontier, is a wild region of 800 square miles, which qualifies it as the largest by far of India's sanctuar-ies. It is very much an unexplored area. Rhino may be present.

30. *Keibul Lamjao*
This is ten square miles of swamp, with a floating mat of humus and vegetation, in Logtak Lake in Manipur, the only patch where the rare browantlered deer survives. Created in 1954, upon the rediscovery of this deer which was previously believed extinct, its inaccessibility has enabled about a hundred deer to find refuge. There are also wild pig and a few hog deer.

31. *Sajnakhali*
Re-crossing into West Bengal in the south, in the vast swamps of the Sunderbans is a great colony of nesting water birds, a fact confirmed only a few years ago. Now the whole area of 140 square miles is a bird sanctuary. It is reached by boat from Calcutta or Port Canning.

The breeding season is from June to August. The main birds

are the spottedbilled pelican, little cormorant, darter, white ibis, blacknecked stork, cattle egret, paddy bird, and little green bittern.

32. *Halliday Island*
A tiny island of 2·3 square miles in the terminal part of the Sunderbans delta. A few tiger, wild pig, and chital are said to be left.

33. *Lothian Island*
This is another terminal island in the Sunderbans, of fifteen square miles, with similar fauna.

34. *Kanha*
This National Park was created in 1955 out of the former Banjar Valley Reserve, in the heart of a wild life region which had few parallels in Asia in the wealth of its fauna. A remnant only is now left of the great forests, grasslands, and wild life.

The Park is of ninety-seven square miles, and is made up of *sal* forest and open grassland. The fauna comprise tiger, leopard, gaur, wild dog, swamp deer, chital, and blackbuck. Poaching has taken great toll, and reduced the swamp deer for which the Park has been famous to 200 head, and the blackbuck to a mere twenty head. Visitors' facilities exist. From July to October, the monsoon months, the Park is not accessible.

35. *Gir*
This 500-square-mile area of thorn scrub forest was upgraded from a Reserve to a Wild Life Sanctuary in 1967. It is world-famous as the last home of the Asiatic lion. The lion survived here through the protection given to it by the former rulers of Junagadh within which Princely State the forest was placed.

The latest census puts the number of lions at 162. The sanctuary is faced with many problems: the slow diminution of the forest through encroachments made into it, the scarcity of the lions' natural prey comprising sambar, chital, nilgai, and wild pig, the vast number of livestock (estimated at 20,000) which graze within it, and the inevitable conflict between their owners and the lions which results.

36. *Taroba*
Taroba, forty-five square miles, is the only sanctuary of any consequence in Maharashtra. It was made a National Park in 1955. Tigers were once plentiful in the tract, but have now become scarce from hereabouts to the south. Leopard, sloth bear, gaur, wild dog, sambar, chital, barking deer, nilgai, and chinkara comprise the fauna. In the lake in the Park are a few crocodiles.

37. *Qawal*
This is one of the three sanctuaries in Andhra Pradesh which deserve mention. Constituted in 1964, it is of 500 square miles, the main fauna comprising leopard, sloth bear, wild pig, sambar, chital, nilgai and chinkara. There are some blackbuck, remnant of the once-teeming herds of this region. An occasional tiger is possible.

38. *Eturunagaram*
Set up in 1953, this is of 314 square miles. Fauna is similar to Qawal. The region generally used to be a centre of big game hunting, tiger specially, but is extensively depleted of wild life.

39. *Pakhal*
The third of this group of sanctuaries, Pakhal was constituted in 1953 and extends over 339 square miles.

40. *Kolamuru*
This is not a properly constituted sanctuary, but deserves inclusion here as the largest pelicanry in India. Spottedbilled pelicans nest in an area of about two square miles in trees amidst cultivated fields, and are fully protected by the villagers, an unusual feature, which has a parallel in Vedanthangal below.

41. *Guindy*
This is a tiny park of trees and scrub in a suburb of Madras, where live a small number of chital and blackbuck.

42. *Vedanthangal*
The best-known bird sanctuary in the south, Vedanthangal is an artificial lake of seventy-four acres. In its middle grow

massed *Barringtonia acutangula* trees, providing nesting sites for a variety of breeding birds during October to March. Prominent among them are the large and little cormorants, darter, spoonbill, white ibis, openbilled stork, grey heron, large, smaller, and little egrets, and night heron.

The sanctuary has virtually existed for as far back as is possible to trace, under the protection of the villagers, before it was declared protected by the Madras Government. It is reached easily from Madras by road.

43. *Ranganthittoo*

This consists of a series of islands in the Cauvery river over about 1·7 square miles, near the city of Mysore. It is another bird sanctuary, where birds breed from June to August. Seen in it are the large and little cormorants, darter, openbilled stork, white ibis, night heron, and cattle egret.

44. *Bandipur*

Bandipur is the inner area of twenty-two square miles of a 310-square-mile wild life park established in 1941 by the then ruler of Mysore. It has a great variety of animals, including gaur, for which it is justly famous, elephant, leopard, sloth bear, wild dog, wild pig, sambar, chital, and barking deer. Tiger used to be plentiful in the Mysore forests, but is now virtually extinct in southern India.

The sanctuary is well provided for visitors, and can be reached by road from Bangalore or Mysore. It can be visited at all times of the year.

45. *Mudumalai*

Contiguous with Bandipur, on the Madras side is the Mudumalai Sanctuary of 114 square miles, formed in 1940. The natural boundary between the two sanctuaries is the Moyar river, but there is free movement of fauna between them. This is a fortunate circumstance as migratory movements of the larger animals have been eliminated almost everywhere in India. Both sanctuaries are on a plateau over 3,000 feet high, but owing to their respective locations with respect to hill ranges, rain falls at different times in them.

Elephant and gaur dominate the fauna, other fauna being

53 Smaller egrets in nuptial plumage, Ranganthittoo Sanctuary

54 Collared scops owl in the Nilgiri Hills, summer
55 Whitebacked vultures approaching to feed on a carcass in the jungle, Mysore

56 Crested serpent eagle, Mudumalai Sanctuary. The nuchal crest is folded normally, and is only displayed if the bird is excited

57 These stone or concrete *machans* are provided in the larger sanctuaries for visitors to sit in and watch wild life. They are, however, generally ineffective due to the surrounding disturbance

58 Old style *machan* on a *sal* tree, Corbett National Park, which I used for watching tiger

leopard, sloth bear, wild dog, wild pig, sambar, chital, barking deer, and mouse deer. Tigers used to be common, but are gone now except for lone survivors. Tourist facilities are good.

46. *Point Calimere*
This area of ten square miles on the sea coast of scrub jungle offers a home for about a thousand blackbuck, the largest surviving concentration in southern India. There are some wild pig and chital. In winter, many migratory water birds visit its coastal swamps, a special attraction being large numbers of flamingoes.

47. *Periyar*
This southernmost of the sanctuaries is of 260 square miles, in Kerala, and was created in 1940 around the artificial lake which rose behind a dam built across the Periyar river in 1900. It is an area of great scenic beauty with wooded hills and valleys and grassland. Visitors are allowed only on the lake, and view the wild life from motor-launches.

Periyar is best known for its elephants, which can be seen almost certainly on any trip round the lake. There are also good herds of gaur, and leopard, sloth bear, wild pig, sambar, and barking deer. Tiger, as everywhere in the south, is practically non-existent. Water birds are common, and the two hornbills, the Malabar grey and the Malabar pied, are also found. Poaching exists as the sanctuary is ringed by plantations, and supervision is difficult because of the terrain.

48. *Mudunthorai*
This sanctuary of 200 square miles in the far south of Madras was set up in 1962, mainly as an effort to provide habitat for any tigers that may have survived. The reserved forests have areas of great scenic beauty, but have been cut up and exploited from development projects and indiscriminate tree-felling. Re-establishment of the tiger in southern India will only be possible through determined and sustained effort.

INDEX